Novels by author:

White Shoulders

Places

Ledges

Blue River

The Paper Man

Different

Missouri Madness

Zed

Shy Ann

Drop 50 & Magnify

Summer of '02

Stuck

Autumn Letters

King of Slugs

To indie writers

September, 2013/1st printing/2,000 copies

Cover Design by Anthony Conrad

"Often wrong...
never in doubt...
so keep writing."

www.michaelfrederick82.com

Photography By: Candace Lea

Indie Writer

Michael Frederick

This book is dedicated to me—
the world's most popular *unknown* novelist.

Foreword

Yes, I'm trying to be funny and cute by dedicating this book to myself. That's because I'm the one responsible for writing, publishing, and marketing all fifteen of my books. You see, I have a good problem: My books are popular, but I'm the only one who knows it. I have forced myself to get over a million readers the hard way. I have placed my titles on the shelves of school libraries and public libraries—one phone call at a time—since 1999.

I have managed to live well and travel more than most writers, all while staying out of the conventional publishing loop and writing whatever I wanted. Only writers should read this book. Whether you independently publish your book or I convince you not to, this book will make or save you thousands of dollars. You're welcome.

3

Finish Writing Your Book

Writing involves not only getting your thoughts down on paper, but it also entails rewriting what you've written and having a willingness to improve your writing each time you go through it. You may go through this process a number of times until it's ready to be given to your editor. I always write my books in longhand and proofread what I've written the next day, making changes here and there. Maybe as much as a year later when the first draft is finished, I'll type the second draft on my computer, making even more changes and inserts along the arduous way of crafting what I believe to be a pretty good story that my editor can polish for me. Then my pages are ready for my independent publishing venture.

I call myself an "indie writer" since I've never been published in the conventional way, and I've never had an agent. I have self-published all of my novels—including this book—in a way that's truly my own. I have never known of any other writers who sell their books the way I have and still do to this day. More about that later.

What must be said early is that this is not a chronological step-by-step way to publish or market your particular book. It's a map I have used that I'm now sharing with you. You will find this particularly useful if you have the freedom to independently publish and market your writing.

I suggest you finish writing your book before you look for an editor (if you don't do your own editing) or a printer. When you're done writing your book, you'll be numb from the experience. After all, you've put your heart and soul into a work of art that nobody else on earth has ever done or could have done the way you have. Congratulations!

Now get it copyrighted with the Library of Congress in Washington D.C. For $35.00 you can register online and protect your work. Make sure your copyright is in the works before you even send it to your editor or anyone to read. Never send your book to friends, relatives, prospective agents, publishers—ANYONE—until your work is copyrighted. The form is easy to fill out, and you won't have to worry about your literary property rights. Ever.

Until you are published the conventional way, you are a writer looking and waiting for validation. Writers wanting to be published "for real" (the conventional way) get an agent, then your agent finds you a publisher. I can't help you with that; I'm out of that loop of validated writers.

Recently, I finished writing my thirteenth novel, *Stuck.* After copyrighting it I sent it to my editor, who is getting it ready so I can submit it to agents for the first time in my writing career. This is also because for the first time I have managed the difficult task of creating a one-page query letter and a two-page synopsis that agents want from a writer before they read the book. These all-important queries and summary letters will tell an agent whether you can write or not. To reduce hundreds of pages and literally thousands of hours of writing and thinking to a mere page or two is no easy task. It requires a sustained focus just like any artist must cultivate, and it is necessary in order to get your work read. I'm telling you this because I am now ready to put that kind of effort into my writing so I can submit my query and summary letter to the big publishers in New York. Since I'm a successful indie writer, I know I have to keep working as if I'll never be discovered and paid to just write like the validated stable of writers are.

If you don't have an editor once you have finished your book, find one. Look online or in the Yellow Pages under "Editorial Services." Or, like me, I found my editor listed under "Secretarial Services." When you call a prospective editor, set up a meeting and request examples of their work—preferably a book like yours they have edited for another writer. At the meeting give the prospective editor your book to read in order to give you an estimate. Meanwhile, you can work on your query and summary letter to submit to agents you can find in *Writer's Market* who are looking for your type of book. This is something I didn't do; I'll explain a bit later what I did.

Once you have written and finalized your two "calling cards," you have given yourself a good chance at getting your book read by an agent. I suggest buying a copy of *Writer's Market,* an annual publication that lists all literary agents and their submission guidelines. Match the agent with the type of books they're representing, along with their submission requirements from writers. It could be that the agency wants a one-page query and a two-page synopsis, or it may want only one or the other. Keep working on both until they are polished and professional. Spend time on them every day, making them as good as possible.

Consider the voice of your story, and make your query and summary fit the story. For example, my novel *Stuck* is a realistic, coming-of-age, historical fiction piece written with a dramatic comedy voice that I want the agent to see in my queries. Below is a sample of my query letter and synopsis for my novel *Stuck*.

Note: The reason I am including these examples of the more conventional submissions to agents is because indie writers owe it to themselves to give their work a shot at getting picked up by an agent. I didn't do this for twelve of my novels. Publishing your own book is a last resort. That'll make sense after you read this book all the way through.

Query Letter:

September _____, 2013

Name of Individual
Name of Publishing House
Street Address
City, ST zip

Dear _____:

A random coin toss made by an encyclopedia salesman. A mail-order Charles Atlas course. Two lazy alcoholic parents. A rich kid named Kaladi. A secret love named Helen. All of these and a thousand other quirky things helped launch Adam Pitt into that rarified air where the ordinary becomes legendary. It was the early 1970s in Pittsville, Missouri—that awful, wondrous season in Americana when talented small-town athletes were "STUCK" facing serious decisions about war, death, and desertion.

When Adam flunks the fourth grade, he needs time to make something of himself. Two generations of Pitts before him had failed miserably in the eyes of the townsfolk. He was the third generation to live in the deteriorating Pitt House. His dead grandfather was a bad memory to the town, and his father was a disgraceful drunk. Adam, the self-labeled "freak from Pittsville," finds solace and acceptance by escaping periodically to Union Station and finding a friend and mentor in a colorful railroad crew chief named Grover Cleveland.

Fresh out of high school, Adam finally has a lower pimple count than his Draft Lottery number. He is terrified of college and equally terrified of being drafted into war. His fears intensify when he and Grover lose a close friend to Nam. Meanwhile, Bobby Taggit—Adam's friend and the son of a proud ex-Marine—deserts the Corps. That's when Adam's escape plan is given to Bobby by old Grover, giving Adam, the walk-on from Pittsville, a new motivation to jump out of the war and into a new life.

Stuck is my thirteenth novel. I have independently published twelve novels and placed them in high school and public libraries in the United States and Canada. This is only the second novel that I have submitted as a query. My readers are both young adults and mature adults because my protagonists tend to be young men coming of age during the sixties and seventies. "Realistic fiction with a unique voice" is what I've heard from readers and librarians when describing my writing.

Thank you for taking the time to consider my submission.

Sincerely,

Michael Frederick

Synopsis:

Certain random happenings had to come together one afternoon in Pittsville, Missouri, to make nine-year-old Adam Pitt an eventual high school track and field legend. The scene had to be set during the 1960s with war on the horizon. Adam had to flunk the fourth grade. A coin toss by an apathetic encyclopedia salesman had to be "heads." A

Charles Atlas mail-order fitness course had to arrive in Adam's mailbox the day his mother bought him a set of encyclopedias. And he had to hate an obnoxious rich kid like Steven Kaladi.

The Pitt House was on a large corner lot; both the exterior and interior of the old Victorian screamed "POVERTY!" The only source of income for the Pitts was their makeshift fireworks stand that was being shut down by the town—fitting justice for a family whose patriarch, Adam's Grandpa Pitt, had shut down his gravel pit in the 1950s leaving half the town unemployed. The family dog Gop is good for a few laughs when you see the mutt's sausage-shaped body doing very little—mirroring his master, Adam's father Bill Pitt. When Grandpa Pitt died, Bill was left a small fraction of his father's money along with the Pitt House. The majority of his old man's money had been left to a church. Bill demonstrated his resentment for his dead father by doing as little as possible to survive and ignoring his father's beloved house, once the grandest house in town.

By the time the chaotic '60s were over, Adam had willfully and creatively used every book in his set of encyclopedias for thousands of hours and was physically ready to launch himself into the national high school track and field record books. He had just one problem: Socially and emotionally Adam Pitt was "stuck." It started at basketball games when Adam would only be put into the game to center jump for the beginning of each quarter. Home and away games were crowded with curious locals wanting to see the self-described "freak from Pittsville" out-jump and embarrass much taller opponents. He'd see them point and make fun of his ape-like long arms and bowed legs as he approached half court with his teammates to begin the game. That's when he'd steal a glance at his motivation—a cheerleader named Helen Bach.

At Adam's first track meet in his sophomore year, he surprised himself and everybody else when he broke two state records in the long jump and triple jump. That's when all the unwanted attention came roaring into his self-consciousness, attacking his low self-esteem like a wolf attacks a lamb. Daily pimple counts, lazy alcoholic parents obsessed with reading daily war casualties, and good rock music—all combined with his grandfather's negative town history—force poor Adam to find a fantasy girl like Helen Bach for his motivation to jump. It's an impossible situation for Adam, though, because Helen loves Bobby even though Bobby broke up with Helen before he left for boot camp; then Helen started dating Steven Kaladi, but Bobby sucker-punched Kaladi so Bobby and Helen get back together; and Helen is pregnant...until she falls down the dark attic steps in The Pitt House.

Throughout the story, Adam steals away to the city to visit his friend and mentor, Grover—a black-skinned railroad kitchen crew chief and retired Red Cap who had a cubbyhole office on a train car stationed in Kansas City's Union Station. "The kid from Pittsville" would come to the massive train station to see a world far different than all-white Pittsville. Grover and Adam have a mutual friend named Reggie, Grover's neighbor and Adam's buddy from the downtown YMCA where they'd shoot hoops on Saturdays.

Adam's small circle of friends from school were Helen Bach; Helen's brother Clark; and Bobby Taggit, Helen's boyfriend and the son of a proud ex-Marine. They are all brought closer together by low Draft Lottery numbers and diminishing time. Adam held two national track and field records, yet he rejected every college recruiter—each one offering a full ride on a brighter stage. The reason he turned them all down? "Because I'm ugly," Adam answered the K.U. head track coach.

Terrified of college and Nam, Adam plans to ride one of "Grover's trains" to Canada before he's drafted; however, when the appointed time arrives he can't leave. He's "stuck"—until he's attacked by his own fireworks and gets enough money from Kaladi's rich father to enroll in school. Anti-war protests on campus increase, Bobby is destined for Nam, and Grover sees his surrogate son Reggie carried home from Nam to Union Station.

Once again, certain random things have to happen in one afternoon when Adam stands on his mark on the long jump runway in the K.U. Armory for the annual track and field walk-on tryout. A crowd has to gather as Crosby Stills Nash & Young's version of the song "Woodstock" plays from #14's tape player; Adam can't scratch; every college track coach in the area has to be interested; and Adam has to see what happened that day he brought Helen to Bobby at Union Station. Everything needs to come together perfectly so that Adam can make this last attempt to save his life and "jump out of Nam."

Wall of Rejection

My independent publishing is far different than eBook publishing. Personally, I like to hold a book in my hands when I read, and at this time I have no desire to read eBooks. Yes, I'm a dinosaur compared to many of you, even though I have two novels on Amazon Kindle, *Ledges* and *The Paper Man.*

When I started writing a new novel every year or so in 1998, eBooks were unheard of—at least by me. Since 1998 I have independently published and marketed my first twelve novels with three new titles coming out in the fall of 2013. Since about 1999 I have been selling my books via telemarketing to thousands of high school libraries and public libraries. Much of that time I have spent 25 to 40 hours a week on the phone selling up to five different titles to one librarian at a time.

This might seem like the hard way to do things, and it is for most writers; however, I like to refer to myself as a "gypsy writer" because I have traveled so much while supporting myself as a writer. And, believe me, I have experienced some pretty grueling circumstances in selling my books—things that are difficult for even me to fathom. Yet my path was only a different path, not unlike anyone who invests their life working a job they love to do every day.

For me, independent publishing begins by finding a competent printing company with experience publishing trade-size paperback books. Look for a printer in your area who can quote you a price for your book. The printer will want to know your word count, approximate number of pages, and number of colors for your covers. Currently, I have my own artist who creates my covers. Some printers have an in-house artist and some don't. I think it's more cost effective to have your own indie artist giving you what you want on your covers.

From my experience, at today's prices a book without illustrations should cost around $1.25 per 100 pages if you order between 3,000 to 5,000 copies. The smaller the number of copies printed, the higher the cost per book. Once you get a quote on your book, including editing and all printing costs, figure out your range of cost per book. A good rule is that you should charge eight to ten times the cost of your book to libraries. That includes all shipping and handling expenses.

If you're on a tight budget and can only raise enough money to have about a thousand copies of your book printed, your cost per book might be as high as $5.00 to $7.00 per copy. But that might be just right for an initial printing in order for you to see how you do before you invest your profit back into another printing.

The most important thing for you to do before you make the decision to print your own book is to develop a plan for marketing and selling your book. I have encountered too many self-published writers who paid thousands of dollars to print their book only to end up with thousands of books stored in their garage. Here's where I can save you money or make you money. There are only a few ways to keep moving your inventory.

The one thing I would recommend that you *do not* do is to sell your book door to door. I call that "direct sales," and that's too hard. I know, because I sold ten thousand copies of my first novel door to door to commercial and residential prospects—one book at a time. That doesn't work unless you're young and have lots of ambition and energy but no brains. It took me two years to sell my first novel this way. At the end of 500 working days selling an average of twenty books per day, I sat down on the curb on a street in Denver and cried for about ten minutes. Then I got up and walked home—which was my car—with less than two hundred bucks to my name. Except for my family and one or two friends, I knew that nobody really cared that I'd sold out all ten thousand copies of my novel *White Shoulders.*

During those two years of selling my book, I believed God would lead me to one good reader who would discover my writing. As time, territory, and inventory passed, I knew I was a better salesman than writer; and that if I kept going to businesses door to door, eventually I would find some profession I wanted to get into or perhaps find a really incredible product I could sell. I thought some manager would discover me and see my potential as a salesman with indefatigable resolve and determination. I had put everything I had into selling that book (even shitting my pants twice while going door to door). I was beyond rejection. I was as serious as a writer can get. In fact, I was too serious.

After getting up and leaving that curb in Denver with my books all sold, I was exhausted and scared because I had zero leads for the future that I could put my energy into. I had faith that God would bring me something for the two years I had endured selling my first book. All the details I remember when selling that book I will save for my memoirs. The point is that I believed in my writing as much as any writer ever has or ever will.

15

After that I never wanted to write another novel again. But like any true writer, I was compelled to keep writing. So from 1982 to 1998 I pretty much traveled aimlessly while writing screenplays. I would live in a town for a month or two doing odd jobs, all the while believing I would be able to sell one of my scripts to Hollywood before I could ever find an agent or publisher willing to back any novel I could write. Yeah, I was jaded, yet I kept writing every day. And I would read everything I could about screenwriting, and I would read novels by writers I admired.

Reading is more essential for writers than it is for anyone else. I should say *slow reading*. Slow down and take the time to see and hear the voice of good writers. See how they tell a story, the poetry and fluidity in the way a sentence moves across a page, all with form and structure like a well-designed and solid home. Stop to reread good writing. Skimming or speed-reading is not for artists. Slow down and find your own voice. At the risk of sounding pedantic: READ and WRITE EVERY DAY.

Assuming you've written your book, rejection stops many writers from rewriting their book or even starting a new book. I was fortunate to create my own hide of leather for handling rejection. Like any actor or artist trying to break into the mainstream of consciousness for their field, writers have to accept and handle rejection in order to stay the course. You have to give up the way it is in order to have it the way you want it. What I mean by that is, keep writing and rewriting. Keep putting your writing out there to agents, and dismiss so-called friends and negative drama that hinder your writing goals. Believe me, if you want to move your writing to higher levels over time with consistent reading and writing, you must take no prisoners. You cannot let the real world of friends and family drain you of the time, energy and creativity that your writing demands. Any serious writer knows that real friends and unconditionally loving family members will support your dream to become a published writer. My way of marketing guarantees you will sell your independently published book to libraries—if you can handle the rejection.

Unless you're young and have boundless energy, hitting the road with your books is not cost effective, especially considering the price of gas these days. I suggest crafting a free web page, for starters. This will give you a place to lead librarians to and will be the beginning of moving your inventory.

If you are not able to devote at least twenty hours a week from Monday through Friday to calling libraries, then my way will not work for you. Don't worry about the phone rejection; I can help you with that by consulting with you for a modest fee when you're ready. I'll provide information on that at the end of this book.

Since publishing and selling your book is important to you, make time for selling your book a priority and make your other jobs and responsibilities work around your selling time. Otherwise, your books will end up being dusty cases of unsold dreams sitting in your garage. Dreams without action are just dreams.

Romancing the Phone

For me, there's no better way to market my books than the telephone. Telemarketing has such a negative image with most people—except the librarians who buy books for a living. I have been calling high school librarians and public librarians for nearly fifteen years. They are, by far and without a doubt, my biggest and best repeat customers.

I am assuming that you—like most indie writers—write fiction or non-fiction stories, and most anything you can write can be sold to a public library. Children's books are sold to grade school librarians, teen books to middle schools, and young adult or adult titles (without graphic sexual content) to high school librarians. If your title is *Painting Cars for Dummies* or *Styling Your Hair at Home*—or some other how-to or self-help title—there are librarians who will buy it, along with a monstrous list of people interested in your book who will buy it directly from you—*if* you call them. That's what I can help you do. More on that later.

It doesn't take long to fall in love with marketing via the telephone once you get consistent sales. Gas and lodging are too expensive for direct sales. And that includes book signings. I'm saving many stories about book signings for my memoirs. I'll just say that if your book is regional non-fiction, you could have some pretty good sales to libraries in the area where your book takes place. But, trust me, that's not going to move your inventory over the long haul. I'm jaded from the poor reception and support I have gotten in my hometown of Sioux City, Iowa. I paid a lot of money for a half-dozen billboards in Sioux City advertising my toll-free number to order my book *Autumn Letters*—a good story that takes place in Sioux City and many of the surrounding communities. After only one miserable sale from all those billboards telling thousands of people that this book was written by a local writer—me—I have since had visions of one day having a "bestseller" plastered on the same billboards with only my bare ass and the words: "KISS MY ASS, SIOUX CITY!" You serious writers will appreciate that, I know.

So don't expect your hometown friends and neighbors to support you. They'll expect a free book, and it will only be awkward when they don't put themselves out to buy your book when you see them down the road. And don't expect sales and honest feedback from friends and family either, because it's not going to happen. I can't remember all the times after first publishing a book that I have been excited to give a copy to family and friends who said they were excited to read it. After assuring me it was a good book, I would ask them a specific question regarding the storyline that they supposedly just had read. The blank look on their face made my joy dissipate into dumbfounded awkwardness and blushing. And all I could see was my bare ass getting bigger on those billboards.

Near the end of this book I'll provide information about how to contact me. You'll need my easy-on and easy-off phone script created for you and your specific book. Don't look now; you really need to read all of this book first. That's how a writer's universe works. You skimmers out there who try to contact me without reading *Indie Writer,* I'll know who you are because you'll have to answer easy questions that only a "real" writer will know after reading this entire book. Skimmers who want shortcuts will only see my billboard; we all get what we deserve.

I wish I had the time and energy to start a publishing company just for independent writers. There are a bunch of us out there with as much talent as any validated writer. Some of you must test this minimal way to independently publish your book. The only way you can lose is if you give up. I used to think: *Man, I could consult with thousands of new writers to get their book out there. I'll be rich!* Now I know: *Man, I could help so many writers by saving them time, money and energy.* Which one sounds full of baloney? Right, the second one. But this is America. We've been programmed to believe in The American Dream—that anybody can get rich if they work hard enough. Baloney! No writer has worked harder and longer than I have to become "successful." You have to work smart by learning to enjoy the process. That has to be enough for you. This way you'll want to improve your writing, and then one day you may get lucky and find someone who sees your talent and thinks they can make money from your work. For most writers, good luck is the residue of sustained effort. I'm not talking about some hack who hits the jackpot online with an eBook about zombies and vampires. Those lucky writers are out there, just like anyone who wins the lottery.

I really got lucky because I wasn't discovered early. I wasn't ready or a good enough writer. I hadn't developed my "voice"—the way I tell a story. During my roaring 20s when I was selling my first book door to door, I just knew that hundreds or even thousands of my first readers were laughing at my books. I could imagine them all getting together for a laugh fest by reading out loud the poor grammar and sentence structure, each reader laughing while pointing out my mistakes on every page. It took me years to stop blushing after I sold out my first novel *White Shoulders*. It was an awful, humbling experience.

So why did I keep going? Because I'm a writer and I believe in my writing. And I'm the only one who has to believe in my work. See, I have over a million readers—and I'm the only one who knows it. That's what keeps me going this way, out of the loop, knowing that I have loyal readers out there.

You must commit to making 50 to 100 telephone calls per day, four to five days a week, Monday through Friday, in order to move your inventory. Don't worry: I'll write a tailor-made phone script for you and your book, a professional pitch that introduces you quick and gets you off the phone without any awkwardness after a rejection. Your calls have to be easy-on and easy-off for you and your prospect, otherwise you'll tire and fade and become too enervated to finish your calls for the day. Just know that you're traveling at the speed of sound, and that half your calls will be to voicemail systems or finding out from receptionists when the book-buyer (usually the library director or librarian) will return. These seemingly insignificant calls are necessary steps that lead you to sales. They're a big percentage of every calling day because most times you'll find out when the library is open and what time is best to reach the librarian or director.

By the way, in case you think you're not the type of person to use the telephone to market your book, emails and direct mailings for orders don't work. Even if you hear that a library is interested in your type of book, you're still an unknown author. Emails don't always get read. In fact, general solicitation emails are ignored for the most part. Trust me on that.

Now once you've made contact with the buyer, she may request that you send them a link to your web page or an email about your book. Don't expect to get a single order from that stalling game. It's far better to give the buyer your web page on the phone and ask her when you can call her back to see about buying your book. Future sales and emails don't pay your bills because they won't move your inventory. Librarians are just too busy these days and too strapped with tight budgets to give your book any consideration. Since libraries get little funding, you're going to get the "no money" response more than anything when you call. So the first thing you have to ask the librarian after introducing yourself is, "Are you buying even one book these days?" Most times the answer is no. Then ask, "Can you tell me when I could call you back?" (Since most librarians are women, I have defaulted to using the female gender.) She'll give you a rough estimate of when she'll be buying books again.

This is where my script comes in. She'll ask you what kind of book you wrote, the genre and who your audience is. You'll be all ready with your practiced, professional response.

If you're one of the few writers out there who wants to do what I do, it is very important that you keep accurate records of every call you make. I suggest you get a library directory or obtain a list from the internet. I often compare what I do to financial guru Suze Orman's seminars. Everybody in her audience is listening and wanting to change their money habits, which she is expertly advising them to do. But what happens a day or two after the seminar? Right. Your hot bath and hopes to make her suggested changes have cooled down to the normal insanity and habits of who you really are, and you're back to where you started. Someday ...

Yes, the phone is your best tool for moving your inventory, and moving your inventory will give you the confidence to keep writing your next book because now you have an audience. One more thing about the phone: Get an unlimited calling plan. You'll need it. Trust me.

Rejection—or even the fear of rejection—stops most new, inexperienced writers from even writing their first book. The fact that I forced myself to become a door-to-door salesman before I started writing seriously is what helped me to peddle my first book without ever considering giving up.

My "wall of rejection" is still there. It is literally, figuratively, and subconsciously all around me. America does not support artists—except for validated actors, singers and musicians, and the stable of writers who easily get reviewed and put on bestselling lists for America's corporate publishers. Indie writers get rejected and dismissed because agents and publishers don't have the time to read every indie submission, even if it is incredibly good. I believe you know this about our country or you wouldn't have read this far. At the very least, after reading this chapter you won't feel so alone for all the unfairness you've already experienced in your writing career. In defense of publishers and agents, they're as jaded and seemingly arrogant as many indie writers are. They know you're not ready for the *New York Times* bestseller list, and they simply don't have the time, patience or compassion to let us know in a constructive manner what can help us improve our work.

The bottom line is there are too many indie writers who don't write well and who submit unprofessional material to agents and small presses willing to read their work. I know because I've been one of those writers not ready for conventional publication for most of my writing career.

I remember when I lived in a cottage near Asheville, North Carolina, and was feeling pretty confident I had nailed a damn good original screenplay titled *The Paper Man*. I had written this perfectly executed, 120-page script with actor Jim Carrey in mind to play this lovesick toilet paper salesman. On his "paper route," this slick TP salesman falls in love with a Native American girl, who eventually dupes her unscrupulous paper man in order to raise money for her impoverished people living on the Pine Ridge Reservation in South Dakota. This story was perfect for a follow-up after Carrey's first Pet Detective film, but he's too old now. If only Jim Carrey had known how many of my readers and librarians have told me how perfect he would have been to play my lead character Harvey Floyd Deason … Oh, well. It was not to be.

During that period I submitted dozens of query letters and entire scripts to agents looking for new writers to represent, and I started a collage of rejection letters on my wall. It had to be ten feet wide and five feet tall, and it covered an entire side of the main room in my little cottage. The most humorous and cynical rejection (which I still have) was sent to me via the self-addressed, stamped envelope I had sent to the agent along with my query. It was literally the size of a slip of paper found inside a fortune cookie with just one word typed on it: Sorry.

Over the years I submitted hundreds of queries and sample chapters of novels and scripts to agents, producers and actors, publishers, and so on. I even turned one page upside-down in the sample work I sent them, and in every single instance it came back with that same page upside down. That told me for certain that my work hadn't been read that far. Of course, my fragile-yet-stubborn ego wouldn't admit that I wasn't ready or, God forbid, good enough. So I got more and more jaded and kept writing. I wouldn't give up. I'd start another novel or screenplay right away when I'd finished one, figuring, *Maybe the next one ... or the one after that.* Eventually, I had multiple submissions going out to all kinds of places. I even sent a few (along with my hard-earned dollars) to those pinheads who charge writers a reading fee, without receiving any real response or honest criticism. At some point after sixteen years of daily writing and occasional agent submissions, and sixteen years after I'd sold out my first novel door to door, I gave up submitting my work the conventional way.

In 1998 I was broke and living near my daughter in Tallahassee, Florida. Seeing her grow up faster than ever when she was in middle school, I was stressed out that I was making so little money from the telemarketing services I was doing from my apartment. I knew I was getting nowhere. Any financially struggling parent knows how stressful life can be just to make ends meet, let alone trying to be creative and write every day. I was so broke that I even had to borrow ten bucks from my ex-wife's husband just to get a little gas and take my daughter to a fast food restaurant. During this stressful period, I was writing a novel I didn't even have a title for. Day after day I spent several morning hours writing up a storm before transitioning into the stressful telemarketing day job. When the calling was finally over for the day, I'd walk around Lake Ella thinking about my title-less second novel. It kept coming to me in wave after wave of clear words and images that moved my storyline along. I knew I was onto something good. No longer was I the same young man with just another five-dollar paperback to peddle; my youthful energy and charisma were gone, and now I had to write something good if I was going to publish a novel again and market it myself.

I had probably ninety percent of my untitled second novel written, and yet I didn't have a location where the story takes place. Just as I knew these things would come to me, I waited. And I waited some more. Until—finally—they did. Ledges State Park in Iowa was the perfect location. I had visited the park one time many years earlier, and that place solved everything. *Ledges* became my second novel. As soon as I could, I loaded a U-Haul trailer with all of my belongings, said goodbye to my daughter, and headed for the place I had to go to see in order to finish my book and make it good.

My drive to Iowa was one long road of confusion. I wasn't concerned with my novel's plot or structure since I'd improved in that area after writing so many original screenplays. It was my marketing of *Ledges* that had to be different. This time I knew I had to use the phone to market my book to indie bookstores, gift shops, and other retailers. From so much phone work I knew I could sell some books here and there telemarketing, plus I would set up prospects on a route who wanted to see my book first. Gas and lodging would be too expensive for cold-calling door to door like I had with my first novel; and I wasn't the handsome young writer who could turn on the charm and sell my books to women. Now I was a very different person—having the energy of a beaten middle-aged man with nothing to show for my consistent writing. But I had another problem: I didn't have any money to pay a printer to print my book.

At Ledges State Park I parked my car and trailer near the entrance and swept through the park like a tornado on two legs, spewing out page after page as I walked the park. I would stop here and there to write longhand, capturing on paper everything my senses could take in.

I left the park and drove to my sister's house in Sioux City, where I rented a room and installed my own phone line. (This was 1998 when telemarketing via cell phone was still impractical and expensive.) I had to come up with some money to print my book, or I would be just another slug doing something other than marketing my dream. I was ready again. I started calling chiropractors around the country whom I had telemarketed for in the past, and I managed to find fifteen or so who paid me $300.00 in advance to get them a few new patients—as I had done before so many times. I hated it, but I was working on a goal. I would call businesses around the chiropractor's office finding and scheduling new patients for each doctor, doing my best to find and schedule a good prospective patient to seven or eight clients a day. Then I would work on a new batch of doctors the next day. It was a stressful juggling act where I had to get lucky quickly so I could find one for the next doctor ... and the next one ... and so on.

During this madness I would make a quick call to a printer in my area, trying to find someone who would work with me in order to get 5,000 copies of *Ledges* printed from my unedited typed pages. Yes, it was maddening. And it was humiliating to be staying with my youngest sister and her husband. All the while, my wall of rejection was growing from the two hundred phone calls a day calling for chiropractors five days a week. I had to keep pounding the phone while hammering out my book on my electric typewriter to the tune of seven or eight pages a night, seven days a week. This kind of stress was making me ugly. My teeth started to hurt when I breathed through my mouth, and my hair was thinning out from my lousy diet and chain-smoking. I was in need of a break; yet kept on, believing I could dial myself out of this mess—if I lived long enough.

As my typed pages of *Ledges* really started piling up, I dialed a number that gave me the lift I needed to make my second book a reality.

The phone I used when I first started calling (just kidding) and the phone I currently use.

Things You Want your Editor and Printer to Know

Everything! I made the mistake of printing my first three titles without the help of a good editor. My first three books were right off my typewriter. Big mistake! I lost a bunch of my early readers because of that.

Make sure your printer shows you other books he has printed for other writers. Look at the quality of the book. Is the binding glued? If so, find another printer. The size of your book will determine the style of binding that should be used. When your book gets over two hundred pages, it's a good idea to look into library-stitch binding so it won't fall apart over time. Just the other day I talked to a librarian in a small-town library in Nebraska. She wouldn't buy my new books because she remembered how a couple of my old books fell apart. Don't use glue to bind your book. Humidity and weather changes will cause the book to fall apart over time if it's glued. However, a small book can use Perma-Binding. Don't accept inferior adhesive binding that will fall apart.

A poorly bound book isn't the only thing to worry about. In the second printing of my book *White Shoulders,* over a thousand copies had pages that were printed upside down. Those were tough to sell. Also, I insist on laminated film covers. That way a water ring or spill will wipe right off.

Three- or four-color covers should give the visual attention that an unknown writer must have. Have your prospective printer show you examples of covers of books he has printed. Fewer colors cost less money to print, but they can cost you many readers if your covers aren't appealing. Readers do judge a book by its cover. Trust me.

Font size and margins should be discussed with your editor. In my first books I had to use a small font to keep my page count down, and it cost me a bunch of readers. Senior readers appreciate a bigger font, but you don't have to have "large print" unless it's a children's book with illustrations. Your editor and printer will know the right size of font for your particular book.

Margins are also important. Make sure your editor knows where your margins should be. I've had margin issues with earlier titles because I wanted to save money by getting as many words as possible on a page. Again, this is something that will cost you readers if they open your book and see margins that are too close to the spine. Looks are important with people, and the look of your book is important to readers. The consumer wants to invest in something that looks professional. You're risking too many returns of your book from libraries if it doesn't look professional.

When your printer has your proof ready for the final read-through before printing, make sure you read your book very carefully and look for typos. Have someone you trust read it too. You'll be surprised at the mistakes you'll catch. Once you sign off that you've read the proof giving the printer authorization to print your book, any typos you have missed will be on library shelves for a long time. And believe me, readers will let you know about them.

I've had letters and emails from readers who pointed out typos and other mistakes—and that was it; nothing else. Editors are good but they can miss things. And it isn't your printer's job to edit your book.

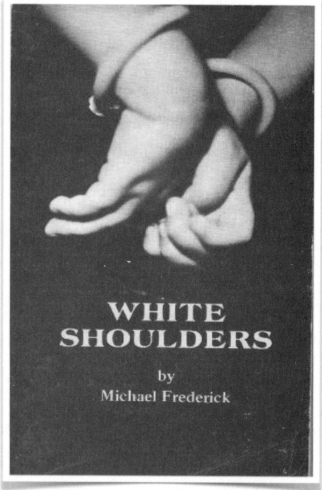

My first book

Gypsy Writer

I got lucky and found a printer in Sioux Falls who agreed to work with me and gave me a good price per copy for 5,000 copies of *Ledges*. The best part was I could pay half down with the other half due thirty days after delivering all two hundred cases of my first printing to me. This news gave me more hope and energy, and I began whittling down my chiropractic obligations by calling in ten to twelve new patients a day.

There comes a moment in every serious American writer's life when they have to give up what they're doing in order to work full-time writing and—as in my case—market their writing. Like a tired old bird that hadn't flown in years, I waddled on shaky legs to the edge of the cliff and stepped out into the terrifying void of unknown space that stops most independent writers. This second leap of faith to peddle a second novel was a fresh oasis of new life into my body and spirit.

By the time my books were delivered to me, I had strategized that my first and best territory for selling *Ledges* would be in and around Boone, Iowa, where Ledges State Park is located. Now I was anxious to use the phone to call prospects from the business listings I had found on my WebTV. I called drugstores, indie bookstores, grocery stores and gift shops in the small towns along Highway 20 leading to Boone, and then dozens of the same businesses in Boone.

I was setting up my stops at a good clip, especially in Boone. On the road my sales were pretty good. I was selling three, six, or even a dozen copies at a time to retailers. I must have sold twenty businesses in Boone copies of *Ledges*. There I was, selling my second novel, and this time signing multiple copies at each business. Instead of the twenty books a day I had sold with my first novel, I had now sold a hundred copies in two days. And for a little more money per copy, too! I thought, *Gee, I'll be able to pay off my chiropractors and printer pretty fast if this keeps up.*

Yes, I was feeling pretty good when I left Boone. I was exhausted when I drove over to Ledges State Park where I had arranged to meet a local newspaper reporter who took my picture at the park and interviewed me. Now I could tell local readers where they could purchase their own copy of *Ledges,* which was a great opportunity to get free advertising for myself and for the outlets that were selling my book. I knew I was selling my book smarter this time, but I still had no clue if readers would buy my book or even like it if they did. I was worried about the small font and the fact that it wasn't edited. But I had a couple favorable Iowa newspaper reviews on the back cover, and I believed the front cover was intriguing enough to get some impulsive and curious readers.

Day after day, then week after week, I kept up a relentless pounding on the phone. I set up a new route out of Sioux City and stayed out on the road selling books to the prospects I called. Letters and emails from readers were coming to me, most of them encouraging me by telling me they enjoyed my book. But then I noticed a pattern in these letters and emails: Almost every single communication had typos and grammatical errors that were in my first two novels. I thought, *Have I been kidding myself? Are these my readers because they write like I do?*

In time, reviews began arriving by mail and on the web. Some were constructive and well-intended. But nothing beat the day I came home from one of my book runs and read an awful, scathing review on Amazon. Mostly it bothered me because it could hurt my sales. I had a new empathy for other professionals subject to public scrutiny—much like an actor in a lousy movie who can't wait until the next film to show improvement. *If* there is a next one.

One such awful, one-star review is on Amazon. I hate it because Amazon has to leave it there for buyers of used copies of my first two printings of *Ledges*. I could tell that the intentions of the woman who wrote the review were negative; but if that pinhead only knew just how much she encouraged me to keep writing, she might have thought twice about her post! Around 2005 I had an edited version of *Ledges* published. Since that third printing came out—a mainline reissue—the edited *Ledges* with the new red cover has had over 200,000 readers from library circulations. It is also doing well on Amazon Kindle and can be downloaded for $3.00 at this time. My point is: learn from your mistakes, and turn seemingly negative feedback to your advantage.

During my selling of my first two printings of *Ledges,* about two hundred Hy-Vee stores in the Midwest were buying two dozen copies of the book at a time, which really helped me move my inventory. But then reorders never came, and some stores would return books to me for a refund. As an unknown writer, I had been required to "guarantee" sales or be willing to offer a refund on unsold books in order to place my books in the stores. Eventually, though, most of my books sold—even though many stores had to reduce their price to get rid of them. All in all, the buying public was a disappointment for me when it came to marketing my books through Hy-Vee. Still, even today about a third of those stores continue to buy my new books a dozen at a time. For the most part, though, I am done selling to retail outlets. The same poor sales through other retail outlets mirrored that of Hy-Vee.

That first winter of calling and selling door to door was wearing on me to the point that I had to have two trips to the emergency room and IV infusions because of dehydration and exhaustion. But at least my debts were paid. I was able to get a nice apartment, living well for the first time in a long time. And yet I knew I was missing something—either a new market for my books or a way to market them—because I was having to drive farther and farther away from my home base to find new territory. Just as I had when selling my first book, I had to keep moving to find a new territory that could sustain me, mostly because retail outlets were a hard sell if they couldn't actually see my book.

I decided to move to Phoenix, Arizona. Not long after that, I had my second printing of *Ledges* delivered to me, which was another five thousand copies. I kept the same cover and didn't have an editor yet, but at least I had a printer who would take half down and the balance thirty days later.

Then I had a huge breakthrough. I started calling public libraries after buying a two-volume set of R. R. Bowker's *American Library Directory, 1999-2000 edition*. This invaluable resource listed the phone numbers, addresses, and contacts for some 27,000 public libraries in the United States and Canada. Each state's towns and cities were alphabetized. Since I'm from Iowa, I started my new book-selling campaign there. And as with any presidential race, I knew I had to do well in Iowa or the other states could be increasingly difficult.

Since I have traveled America during most of my adult life, I was able to help myself when calling libraries around the country. I could truthfully market myself as a Nebraska writer or a South Dakota writer or even a former Indiana writer. I could say the same for California, Oregon, Washington, Arizona, Virginia, Michigan, Florida, and so on since the only state I didn't live in at one time—even if I was only living in my car—was Alaska. Yes, I was a self-labeled "gypsy writer" when I lived in my car; I was young and poor and filled with wanderlust, and I logged millions of miles of asphalt and gravel while experiencing my country. My point is that my traveling established in me a connection with these librarians I was calling for the first time. The same held true for retailers. Stable people like their area, and it always helped me sell books when I mentioned that I had experienced their part of the country.

Now my new market became public libraries that, for the most part, were in small towns. I realized I was missing out on half of my possible readers and libraries by not placing my books in the collections of bigger city libraries. Don't get me wrong; I did call the bigger libraries. But I found out from thousands of marketing attempts over a decade that the bigger libraries have too much red tape for someone like me, an independent novelist. The bigger libraries want reviews from source books like *Library Journal, Booklist,* and *Publisher's Weekly.* These bigger libraries rarely buy from independent (self-published) writers. Librarians and collection development staff in libraries of bigger cities—or even regional libraries in smaller towns that select and buy books for several branches—will only buy from vendors or distributors like Baker and Taylor, Follett, and the like.

Getting reviews for your book … Don't get me started! I'll have more on reviews in a chapter later. I'll tell you, though, that I have submitted my novels to these source books, and I never did get one of my titles reviewed. Granted, most of my books weren't good enough to get raving or even positive reviews, so maybe it was a blessing in disguise that none of my titles were deemed worthy of any response. But at the time I resented being ignored. I felt like I was being kept out of the loop of conventional writers.

Getting published and reviewed is like politics. There's an established system in place that keeps indies out of the game. So get your query letter and two-page summary as polished as you can. And if you're not sick of thinking about your book, be willing to rewrite it after leaving it alone for some time. Once you begin again, remember that Hemingway advised writers, to wit: It's better to stop writing when you're going good because it's easier to pick up from there; that way the rest of your day goes well, too.

Be careful what you dream; you might get it. So many writers I have talked with over the years talk about writing their book "someday." I could never tell those writers the truth: "Dreams without action and hard work are just dreams. Stop being just another dreamer."

Good looking young door to door salesman...and me now.

Tricks of the Trade

Hemingway also had advice for writers who think they need the right time or place to be creative and write: The only thing a writer needs to have when he writes is his mind.

If you're in the throes of writing your book, congratulations! You've managed to go further than most people who simply "think about" or "want" to write their book. I suggest you write about what you know and develop the "characters" you know. The best character you know is you. All my characters are a reflection of me and what I've experienced and can imagine. My protagonists usually start out as the boy I thought I was—at one time or another. Max Perkins, the famous editor of many accomplished writers, said, "The best part of every man is the boy in him."

I can't imagine telling any story without showing the early lives of your characters. I'm confident that if I can get my readers to love the boy, they'll like the man—or at least understand him. At the risk of sounding like some pedantic sprout head, I suggest you get in touch emotionally with the characters who drive your story.

It's not important how old you are or how old your characters are, or even if you're selling "tricks of the trade" for Wall Street investors; you must connect with yourself and relay that real connection to your readers to establish something we all have in common: our youth.

So many writers have told me, "I have this story I want to write, but I don't know where to begin." The first thing I say to new or young writers is that there are three parts to every story: a beginning, the terrible middle, and the ending or a climax leading up to a resolution. Young American writers (myself included) see visually because we've been visually stimulated and entertained by film and television our entire lives. We've been programmed over decades to see and read about happy endings for the most part, or at least a resolution or ending that surprises us. I'm not suggesting that's good or bad; I only know that my most popular books have tied up all the characters and loose ends to a satisfying conclusion.

You should know where your story begins. Make your first sentences as good and interesting as you can, if only because you're a new indie writer and your readers will read the beginning of your book and decide before the end of the first page if they want to read the rest of your book.

So let's say you know where your book begins. You also have to know where it's headed. You don't have to know the ending. My best books have surprised me along the way, sometimes all the way to the end. That's a good feeling when your book leads you to places you never imagined. When that happens I know I've developed my characters and storyline with a flexible foundation that can surprise me and my readers.

The hardest part of any novel is what I call "the terrible middle." I liken it to any long trip that's going to take you thousands of miles to reach your destination. At first you're excited to be on your way, to be moving along familiar territory; but then comes that unknown part of the journey when you have to find a way to enjoy the ride and make the scenery interesting enough to keep you from being bored or falling asleep. When you see that you're nearing your destination, your energy level picks up and once again you're excited because you're closing in on the place you've imagined for so many miles.

My travel analogy point is that the whole trip needs to be enjoyable from beginning to end. If you get tired of writing or experience what some writers call "writer's block," take a rest. Get away from it and come back to your story the next day with a fresh mind. Indie writers like myself have a tendency to force words on the page rather than see the story not moving while another day goes by. After years of writing every day, I am comfortable to let the words come out of me and trust that my story is going to keep moving without getting lost.

Rewriting is not a trick of the trade; it's an unwritten law for any serious writer. Any book I have stubbornly, lazily, or ignorantly refused to rewrite at least two or three times has never been as successful as the ones I have rewritten. REWRITE!

The cost of your book is important. I'm not talking about eBooks or other ways to print your book one copy at a time. I know about how much you should pay for your book if it's printed by a reputable printer. Depending on your page count and the number of copies printed (without illustrations), you should get a quote for a few bucks a copy *if* you don't live in an expensive metro area like New York City or Los Angeles. Keep in mind that your quote may not include your artwork or freight charges if you have your books shipped to you. I suggest picking up your books at your printer's location in a U-Haul or van. I have saved thousands of dollars every printing by doing just that.

My operation is a little different. I have pretty much developed and implemented the best system from trial and error as an indie writer. Since I have so many libraries to call when my new books come out, I start calling them nine or ten months before my books are ready, taking orders for two to three books that I'm still writing. I start by calling my best libraries in December or early January because these are the easy sales and are as good as standing orders. I always call them and make sure the same librarian who has been buying from me is still doing the buying. Some librarians retire or take another position, move, or even pass away. Every time I call librarians to preorder my new books, I never fail to lose dozens of libraries because of such changes. Also, the new buyer doesn't know that my books were preordered by the time my books arrive in October. Every now and then even some of my best librarians return my books to me because they don't remember that I called them six to ten months earlier. That's why I've started asking each buyer for a "password" I can put on my invoice, such as the buyer's favorite color or a beloved pet's name—anything to remind them when my books arrive in October that I had called them.

It really tees me off when I get my new books returned to me from a new librarian who didn't order my books, since all she has to do is look to see that she has several of my titles in her collection and verify the order with the previous buyer whose name is on my invoice. When I do get books returned by a librarian, I remove that library from my call list. I take it personally because I work hard to place my books there, and I know that my loyal readers at that library will read my new books. Not to mention, one of my favorite rewards is knowing my new books are on the "new book table" after two years of writing and selling and the myriad little things it takes to put two books out into this world.

Another "trick"—which is probably my most important one—is to effectively juggle and balance my personal life with my writing. I used to think that thousands of hours of solitude would organically manifest into better writing. It doesn't work that way—unless you're in prison or terminally ill. Luckily for me, I have never experienced either of those challenging situations. It is imperative for you as a writer to have a life outside of your characters; otherwise, as the storyteller you will lose the sustained voice of life and energy it takes to write a fifty-thousand-word (or more) manuscript. For writers especially, some days are better than others. There will be days when people or situations will impose on your writing time. That's why many writers distance themselves with a solitary lifestyle. When life happens to you, find a way to go with it and resolve to write more the next day. After you experience a pattern of resistance from external or internal influences, know that this distraction or interruption will make you a better writer. Remember that life will never fail to help you become a better writer, and the people who really love you and support your writing will not impose on you intentionally during your writing time. Most of all, be fiercely protective of your special time to write, and make certain any distractions are not masked as your own procrastination. Writers write.

By letting you know that I will consult with you regarding independently publishing your novel (in book form), I don't believe I'll regret that since only a few of you will actually want help in that direction. I'm aware that this book will more than likely turn most of you indie writers off because of the work involved in marketing your book this way. As is the case with me, your long-term goal might be to eventually have a conventional publisher do all that work for you. It could happen. People win the lottery every day. Just remember: the more you read, write and rewrite your book, the more you improve your chances of an agent or publisher seeing your book as their winning ticket.

My books are in libraries and my books are on Kindle

My Situation

Talk about unique, here is my situation: I have published my first twelve novels and have three more books likely to join the others on library shelves in October 2013. It is only because I have personally called the librarian or buyer in your library that my new books are in your hands.

Stuck is my "lucky thirteenth" novel and presently the one I feel good about—more so than any other book I have written. *Stuck* was never "stuck" for me; it seemed to be too easy for a thirteenth novel. My editor thinks it's my best book after editing it. I can tell it must be pretty good because she hasn't complained about any serious revisions or cutting—only a few minor inserts regarding character development.

My best friend is my girlfriend. She has spent several hours scouring the internet and *Writer's Market* for agents. We have submitted a *Stuck* query letter, summary, and sample chapters to several. Whatever the agent's submission guidelines are, we have satisfied some thirty of them. Five or six have responded with no interest, and we're hopefully waiting for a positive response from one agent who wants to read the entire manuscript. I'm confident one of them will see the story as a real and rare gem and want to represent me. That is, until I explain "my situation." Here's how I expect that conversation will go:

"Michael?"

"Yes!"

"This is I. M. Shyster with Shyster and Sons Literary Agency."

"Hi!"

"We've read *Stuck* and would like to represent you."

"Gee, that's good news ... except I must tell you my situation."

"Yes?"

"I've self-published my first twelve novels and sold them myself via telemarketing to thousands of public and high school libraries in the U.S. and Canada. Mr. Shyster, for fifteen years I've been selling my books to libraries. On January 2, 2013, I began calling my libraries and pre-selling *Stuck*, along with my other two new titles. I have been selling and writing up orders and filling out shipping envelopes like gangbusters in preparation for shipping all my orders at once at the beginning of October."

"I see."

"I have to have one of two things Mr. Shyster: First, you have to find a publisher willing to give me a six-figure advance if that publisher doesn't want me selling *Stuck* to all my libraries. Keep in mind, I only sell my trade-sized paperbacks to small-town libraries for the most part. I know I have laid a foundation for potentially a bigger retail market by consistent telemarketing for fifteen years. The second option is, I keep selling my book my way to my existing libraries only, without any retail calling on my part whatsoever."

"Well, Mr. Frederick, even though option one would be good for both of us, it's unlikely. And the second option ... well ... I just don't see that happening."

That's how I think that will go. I understand it because they want to sell *Stuck* to all of my libraries too. And if they don't see it my way, I expect I'll be the one who sold this book to your library. *

Over the years I have learned to resent such terms as "vendor," "jobber," "distributor," "Baker and Taylor," "Barnes & Noble," "Follet," and the like. These terms are also known as "the middleman." I have cut out the middleman by directly selling my books to libraries. If you self-publish and put your book in the hands of these middlemen, you're only doing them a favor. They'll want you to conform to their red tape by shipping them a test batch of your book—at your expense, of course. Then if any books are sold, they'll send you a commission check every three months for forty to fifty percent of the retail price. I'm not certain of the exact figures, but I do know I'm not interested in consignment and having to keep track of where all of my books are. I think that's a good way to go broke, and the whole system is anything but proactive. I look at it this way: Since we've allowed banks to get away with not paying interest to depositors, my books are by far the best return on my investment that I can get.

49

There's another important thing I can help you with if you decide to use my consulting services, and that is determining how much you should charge libraries and retailers for your book. If you call or email me for a consultation, I will have you send me a copy of your book that I will price for you. I will consult with some of my librarians and find out what your price range should be for public and school libraries. This is something most newbie indie writers could do on their own, but I'm there for help if needed in that area. Later chapters will cover more on schools and other things like barcoding and W-9 forms—little things you'll have to do that are simple and yet unknown to indie writers.

*By late May 2013, I have not received one positive response from my queries to agents regarding my new title *Stuck.*

My 13th Novel

Reviews

These are other words I have come to resent over the years as a struggling indie writer: *Booklist, Library Journal, Publisher's Weekly,* and so on. These are the source books that librarians read to find out if a book has positive reviews. With money and budgets so tight, I understand that librarians have to be careful what they buy, and they certainly don't have the time to read every book—or many books at all, for that matter.

Many of my loyal readers are small-town librarians who read my books and enjoy them. I always enjoy talking to them; they lift my spirit. Funny how my books do well in those libraries.

Back to these aforementioned "bad words." Reviewers have submission guidelines, and over the years I've shied away from submitting my work to them—even though I realize I'm missing out on hundreds if not thousands of sales by doing that. I have my doubts about whether any of my books warrant a positive review from source books; and only one bad review could cost me sales or, even worse, returned books. I don't trust them to review an independent writer with the same fairness conventional or established writers get. That assessment may originate from my cumulative insecurities from choosing to live off my circulation in libraries rather than risk being "attacked by the herd," if you will.

The heart of any resistance on my part comes from having a high school education with average grades. Rather than go through an overrated post-secondary education system and be saddled with debt, I would rather read *Elements of Style* several times. I really couldn't tell you any of the rules of proper grammar, except for the most rudimentary. Over the years I've had various editors and college students edit my books and recall being embarrassed by their corrections without understanding why the corrections had to be made in the first place.

Even if *Stuck* is rejected by every agent I submit it to, I'll keep writing—and, I hope, improving—with every intention of continuing to self-publish. Over the years I have found from library circulation figures given me by librarians that my books have been read by over a million readers. My situation is I'm the only one who knows that my books are popular in thousands of libraries in the U.S. and Canada. It may take finding an open-minded small press publisher to recognize that I have already built an incredible platform for my titles to really take off in the big leagues of retailers and metropolitan libraries.

Knowing what I know, I may have to settle for small-town newspaper reviews that mean very little to most book buyers. More than likely, though, I won't look for any reviews. When you choose to follow your own path of independent publishing, you will have to work as if you'll never be recognized or accepted into the herd of conventional publishing. Don't worry about that. Your readers will sustain you now and then; however, your biggest fan has to be you. You are the only person who can keep you motivated day after day over the long journey as you sit down to write the things that only you can say in your own unique way.

A word of caution: Beware of *Publisher's Weekly*, since they charge a fee of $150.00 to review a book. Not for me!

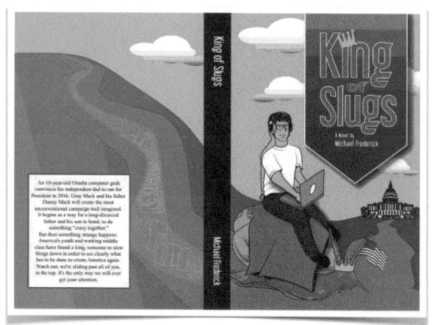

My 14th Novel

Double Your Market with Schools

If your book can be sold to public schools, you have substantially increased your market for moving your inventory. If your book can be sold to librarians in grade schools, middle schools or high schools, you'll reach an ever-repeating audience of new readers and librarians who will help keep your writing juices flowing and your inventory moving.

Even though budgets are tight and little money is spent on new titles, you will still find incredibly generous librarians who will give your book a chance in their libraries. But after several years of raking my public library directories, I had to find another big market. Thank God for public high schools! I realize that a true artist must write what he or she wants to create; however, sometimes adaptations must be made to accommodate new markets. I adapted my writing over the years to include young adult readers in high schools in order to double my libraries in the U.S. and Canada without one single professional review. That meant I had to tone down my writing for my new and younger readers.

You can see my dilemma. I had been writing novels with adult protagonists and characters in most of my books, so my books were categorized and shelved in the "adult fiction" sections of my public libraries. My market adaptation strategy was a blessing in disguise, since now I prefer to write my novels with teens and young adults as main characters—or at least more than I have before. Now my stories can take place in the 1960s and '70s. That way I can keep my adult and senior readers, since most of them recall that era and can enjoy reading about young characters in a genre better categorized as "historical fiction."

One of the more important discoveries I have made is now I realize that life was and is more thrilling when you're young. This is partly because youth go through new life situations and conflicts that have more impact on their lives, compared to more mature adults who are settled in and have far fewer inclinations for adventure and risk-taking. Who really cares if a middle-aged character is heartsick and lonesome or going through tough times? But youth—now, that can be thrilling! And a writer can go back to the time when they were young and their character was being formed. To me it's justification. I feel like now I'm cashing in on my years of aimless wanderlust, those years when I resisted stability and the security many people get from staying put.

Since libraries are not being funded like they used to be (and should be), there's no really good time of the year for an indie writer to call school libraries or public libraries. Spring used to be a good time to call school libraries, but nowadays I have to keep pounding the phone during the entire school year and eventually get lucky here and there.

Keeping good records on callbacks is important, and you should be sure you follow up with librarians like you tell them you will. But don't expect them to open up their checkbooks *en masse*.

You'll come to find with most callbacks that libraries still won't have the money they thought they were getting; and if they did get the money, they probably spent it as fast as they could.

I have learned from my experience that there are so many details you'll have to pay attention to that it's impossible to put them all down in any practical order. That's why as I write this book, I am anxious and eager to consult with you indie writers (for a fair fee) in order for both of us to prosper.

In the late '90s I discovered an excellent market niche in calling public libraries and thought I'd found an endless gold mine. That lasted until 9/11. That was the day I slammed my fax machine to the floor of my apartment and threw one of its shattered parts through my closed kitchen window. Aside from the obvious act of horrific terrorism, I knew that was the end of the good times for selling my books to libraries. That day was the beginning of my "shock" and the end of my "awe" for the good thing I had going. I knew from that day on I was headed for far fewer sales and wholesale rejection. Yes, the *lack* of money is the root of all evil; even the most greedy people fear they'll never have enough of it. Since "war" is the king of fear and greed, things like funding for books and libraries all but stops.

As I was writing this, I had a thought: *What if none of you indie writers reading this book wants to market your book like I do?*

One good thing about marketing your book to libraries or your specialty market is there are always plenty of calls to make; you'll always have a job if you do this. You can buy an accurate list of all the schools in the U.S. (including phone numbers and addresses) for a few hundred dollars. If you ask me, it's well worth it. And for you indie writers on a shoestring budget, here's another trick of the trade for testing the waters before you spend any money on directories or lists: From the internet get yourself a small sample calling list of public libraries and public schools around your area. With the easy phone script I custom create for you and your book, you will quickly discover that you are ready to invest in a directory. The success of my approach will give you the confidence you need, and you will realize that you can get the sales you need to sustain your business. The best part is, you will look forward to every new day of calling as I do. Calling libraries closer to home will break the ice for you and increase your chances of selling your book, which is so important when you begin your marketing.

Your greatest obstacle to calling any school library will be reaching the librarian. Again, with tight budgets teachers are busier than ever. Chances are the first time you call, you'll get her voice mail. Go ahead and leave your name, number, and a very brief blurb about your book; then close your message by (slowly) leaving your website address. A website helps you by giving the librarian something to look at *if* she's interested. Again, be sure to keep an accurate log of the organization you called, who you spoke to, the date you called, and the outcome of the call. For the above example, I would make a note on my log that I left a voicemail with my webpage and note the date (W/VM 10/22). If I talked to her in person and left her my web address, I'll note that on my log (W/T 10/22). Develop a system that is easy for you to use, and stick with it consistently.

When you first call a school and get the busy school receptionist, try to get the (head) librarian's first name. The key is you must be quick about it, since busy receptionists are quick to put you through once they hear you want to talk to the librarian. My phone script for you will cover these little details that add up to smooth calling.

Say I find out that the head librarian's first name is Mary and I get her voice mail. I note her name on my log and the result of the call. I'll give busy Mary a few days to check out my webpage, then I'll call back and ask, "Is Mary the librarian in now?" Oftentimes the school receptionist knows whether she's in or not. Many times they put you through to the voicemail again because Mary might be screening her calls and not pick up if she doesn't know you. After getting bounced around like this, you'll learn to ask the receptionist on the first call if Mary is in *now*. If not, find out when Mary's prep period is or a time when she's free to talk because she's not in a classroom. I don't want to leave a second voicemail; I want to find out when I have the best chance of Mary picking up her phone.

Experience on the phone has taught me not to leave messages on the voicemail because Mary doesn't know me. Since I don't return calls to people who I don't know when they leave me voicemails, I conclude she won't call me. Busy teachers screen their calls. That's why on the rare occasion I do leave a message on her voicemail, I want it to really count. I might say, "I'm an author in Nebraska. This call is about my books for boys." Then I'll leave my webpage. The same is true when I have the receptionist on the phone for the first time. I may say the same thing I said on my voicemail message, that I'm an author and it's about my books for boys. When the receptionist calls the librarian and relays that message, the librarian may take the call *if* she's looking for books for boys.

Many times the receptionist will ask you if you'd like to leave a message on the librarian's voicemail. Yes! Do it! Then call her back later and see if she's looked at your webpage. Just remember this: Good leads are glad you called.

Considering all the responsibilities and the workload of school and public librarians, they are more than willing to help you along your marketing journey with your book. In time they will teach you all the things you should do to place your book in libraries. I'll save you thousands of calls before you find out the hard way the best way to sell your book to these media specialists.

I could go on and on about certain things you'll be asked by librarians. Learn from every call, keep good callback notations, and listen for those helpful librarians who are glad you called. They're out there. Trust me.

One of my many high schools.

Tossed, Lost, and Returns

These are three negatives that will be a part of any product you are selling—especially when it's a book from an unknown author. I'll cover these as quickly and painlessly as possible; however, you have to know these three negatives will happen and they will be a disappointment.

Tossed

These are the invoices librarians will lose when your book arrives. You'll find this out when you call thirty to sixty days after you've mailed your book and your check hasn't arrived. After publishing twelve titles, I still get public and school librarians who lose or misplace my invoice. It's frustrating and happens too much. You'll end up emailing or snail mailing another invoice.

This is a good place to mention that you should ship your books via "media mail" through the United States Postal Service. You can use "library rate" to save a few cents, but many postal clerks are not familiar with USPS rules for shipping books via library rate. Besides, the price is so close to media rate that I don't bother to inform these clerks otherwise. I have run into enough hassles with clerks to learn that it is better to stay away from library rate for my books. Just ship your book media mail.

You should also have a two-part invoice (original and one copy). The original should be enclosed with your book in a bubble mailer with the invoice copy filed in your alphabetical filing system. Never use a plain flat manila envelope to ship your book because the machines used by the USPS to sort mail can be as rough on books as primates peeling bananas.

This is also a good place to let you know that you will have to do some overdue invoice collecting when your check is late. Because of the lack of money, withholding is a common practice with five to ten percent of my libraries. I suggest you put "net 30 days" on your invoice, knowing it could take up to sixty days to receive your check. Some libraries pay bills only once a month after the invoices have been approved for payment by the Board of Directors at their monthly meetings. Depending on when your invoice arrives at the library and how it coincides with the board meeting schedule, compounded by the sluggish mail system, it could take a couple months to get paid.

Lost

That's when you call a librarian about your late check and she tells you she hasn't received your book yet. She'll want to look around for your book, and more often than not she'll find it still in the shipping bag you sent, unopened and stacked in a pile near her desk. Again, this happens about one to three percent of the time.

But there is also another kind of "lost." Every once in a while you'll call the librarian about your outstanding invoice, and she lets you know that the post office must have lost it because she can't find it. Right then I ask if I can send another book to her to replace the lost book, and she usually tells me to do that. I know what you're probably thinking, but I'll just say that librarians are honest people. If they say they didn't receive your book, more than likely they're telling you the truth. I only know of a few librarians (not worth mentioning) who have lied to me about my "lost" book.

In these cases I have found it isn't worth it to go to the post office to fill out a form to have them look for your lost book. They'll never find it because they're "too big to succeed" in such an endeavor. Sometimes the post office will send me my empty, damaged mailer with a note about how sorry they are. Don't waste your time and energy by filling out that form. But do take that form with the damaged package to your post office, and they're pretty good about not charging you postage to mail the replacement book. Usually.

Returns

This is the best of the three negatives because at least the librarian returned your book to you, so now you can resell it to another library—as long as it hasn't been damaged in the mail. If I can't resell the returned book, I'll give it away to someone and sign it to my new reader knowing I've just brightened someone's day. And maybe gain a new loyal reader in the process.

Returns used to be the most dreaded thing in my early days of marketing my book. Oftentimes I would get a note on my returned invoice from the librarian stating that she didn't think my book was suited for her library. In other words, it wasn't good enough or up to her standards.

The appearance of my early works usually was the reason my book was returned. Very seldom did the librarian read my book. I know that my margins were too close to the edge of page, or the font was too small because of my shoestring budget. I had to get as many words as possible on a page to cut costs. And *if* she did get to read a page or two, it wouldn't take her long to notice the lack of editing in my early titles.

For whatever reason a librarian returned my book—and often none was given—I wouldn't call that librarian back for five years or more. When I did call back after several years, time stepped in and good things had happened. The best thing that happened was I had kept writing and selling out every printing of every title consistently. Another good thing concerned *Ledges,* my second novel. I was able to finally have a third printing edited and a new cover designed (a mainline re-issue). I began selling it to schools like gangbusters with terrific circulation figures. Then when school was out for the summer, I was able to call many of those public libraries that had returned my unedited first and second printings of *Ledges,* which I could quickly and accurately identify from my notations in my library directory. I had a few things working for me this time around: time and change, for example. I found that many of those librarians had moved on or retired, and I now had a chance to start fresh with a new buyer. I also had a new book or two I was selling along with the new and improved *Ledges.* On top of that, I was getting great positive feedback from readers in schools and public libraries almost daily.

Consequently, I was now selling two or three different titles to the libraries that had returned the old *Ledges* to me. Sometimes—depending on my inventory—I would sell four or five different titles at a time. Many of those libraries are still with me today and happy to order my new titles when they come out. I was thrilled to turn those once-dreaded returns into positive sales by waiting until I had new titles and the "old" librarian was gone. Of the librarians who had returned my books earlier and were still there when I called years later, many remembered me because not many writers call them consistently like I have for fifteen years. Many of them rejected me numerous times over the years. But then a new librarian would take the place of the old one and buy my books, giving me a chance to place my books in her collection and on the new-book table. Thank God for new voices!

This is a good time to mention that I believe October 1st is the best time of year to publish your new book. Smaller public libraries usually start a new fiscal year then, and some schools are still buying at a good clip. (I have found, though, that most schools like to buy books in the spring for the beginning of the next school year.) January 1st would be my second-best time to come out with a book because public libraries start a new year, and public schools are starting to buy for the coming spring.

These three negatives I have mentioned will always be there for independent writers. Accept them and keep calling your prospects. Even if your book is a how-to book about restoring cars and you bought a list of businesses in that particular line of auto restoration, you'll still get these three negatives now and then. That's why it is important to flexibly price your book higher than what your known or fixed expenses are.

Book Signings and Other Disasters

Don't get too excited about book-signing events unless you enjoy hearing yourself talk to a bunch of dead-faced strangers who have nothing better to do than listen to an unknown writer talk about a book that they don't value.

Now, I'm not talking about a local historical non-fiction title or a true crime story that might be of interest to some locals in libraries within a hundred-mile radius of where the event happened. You could get a good turnout—*if* your signing isn't taking place during an athletic event or close to their next meal. In other words, book signings are not a proactive way to consistently move your inventory. And I'm not saying anything negative about signings if you've only had a few hundred copies of your book printed, because then you can obviously take your time and find out just how well you can sell your book at signings.

Indie bookstores, grocery stores, swap meets, and plenty of libraries—I've done them all. I've found out the hard way that most of the people who attend signings in these venues are a little curious about your book, but mostly they would rather attend a softball game and spend their money on a hot dog and a few beers than help some indie writer by buying his book.

It seems like so long ago when I first bought my Minnie Winnie RV for my much-anticipated book-signing tour. I was ready to let the public come to me at my scheduled library signings. I had called all over Oklahoma and Kansas and set up over thirty book signings in a forty-day period in the middle of summer. They were intimate settings in small-town libraries where my books were circulating well and where librarians were willing to buy me one meal. In some instances I was fortunate to have one who would pay for a motel room for one night. Those librarians who were providing me a place to stay were greatly appreciated because sleeping in an RV during the heat and humidity of summer in the Midwest can be quite uncomfortable; and the combination of high gas prices and very cramped living conditions adds more financial stress and physical discomfort.

Of all those library book signings, only one in Palco, Kansas, was a success. I'll never forget driving into that little town of perhaps a few hundred people in northwestern Kansas. There in the middle of the desolate "Main Street" was my eight-by-ten flyer I'd sent to all the libraries to post, which announced the date and time of the signing in their library. My flyer was attached to a waist-high pole that was anchored by a windproof stand (formerly a truck tire). There were secured copies of my flyer facing each direction. Then I saw the old Palco Public Library that was located on the corner. It was housed in one of those old, small-town bank buildings of dark brick that had to be over a century old. It even had a horseshoe pit just behind the building.

To my surprise, the little library was packed with people of all ages who were waiting for me to arrive. I greeted everyone seated with me around a large library table, as well as others on chairs or standing around the main room of the library. There were delicious homemade cookies and punch on the table for what was about thirty to fifty people, including little kids. I talked about their little town first, wanting to know if anything notable ever happened there. They informed me that Palco gets earthquake tremors now and then, which I found incredible considering it is out in the flat sticks of Kansas. Before that signing was over, I had to make two trips to my RV to get more books to sign and sell to my Palco readers.

After the Palco signing, things went back to the normal insanity of one or two books sold at my lonely little table-and-chair setup at the remaining scheduled signings in Kansas. Thank God I was smart enough to bring my *American Library Directory,* along with a stack of old invoices. Every chance I got, I was making calls from my RV on my cell phone's unlimited calling plan. At least that way I was able to collect on past-due invoices and consistently sell books and ship them from a local post office every day to keep my flow of income coming in when I'd get skunked at signings.

Another example of what I *thought* would turn out to be another Palco was in Bryson, North Carolina, at a rather nice-sized library. About sixty people were seated on folding chairs to see and hear me and another writer. I was living in Asheville, North Carolina, at the time, so I'd billed myself as an "Asheville writer" on my flyer to help my sales. The other writer at the event wasn't a hard act to follow because I nearly dozed off while waiting for my turn behind the podium. I can remember keeping myself awake by going over my own presentation as the old writer went on and on about his hiking experiences on the Appalachian Trail with his dog Sleepy. I kept telling myself, *I know I can sell everybody here at least one copy of my book* Missouri Madness *if I can wake them up after this guy shuts up.*

Finally, it was my turn. Before the smattering of applause was over, I began handing to the audience laminated copies of newspaper articles about the true crime I had researched that took place in Bath, Michigan. The old black-and-white photographs of the Bath School Disaster of 1927 immediately grabbed and held their attention. And rightly so. It was America's biggest mass murder until the Oklahoma City bombing, and very few had ever heard of it.

I found out about this incredible crime when I was selling my first novel door to door in Arizona and California. Somehow I found and bought a rare used copy of a book about the disaster written not too long after it happened. At first I felt and thought it was something too terrible to write about; yet there I was in a small-town library in North Carolina displaying on the table four copies of my novel *Missouri Madness*. They were right there next to me by the podium as my captivated audience passed along my newspaper articles on this unbelievable yet true disaster. I had only thirty minutes, so I hurried along my audience by telling them, "Please don't read the entire article, folks. Just skim the headlines and pass it on. I only have thirty minutes to cover a lot of ground."

As an experienced salesman, I knew I had their attention; yet there was a part of me that believed I was exploiting an awful tragedy for personal gain as I rounded up and collected my laminated "attention getter." I could see my audience squinting and staring at the ominous cover of *Missouri Madness*. (More on covers later.)

"Have any of you heard of the Bath School Disaster of 1927?" I asked my audience.

Nothing but silence.

"That was one of the things that compelled me to go to Michigan to research this disaster. I'll give you a summary of what happened: On May 18th, 1927, a madman and local school board member meticulously planned to blow up the Bath School with dynamite because he was enraged over a recent vote to raise property taxes in order to increase funding for the school. It was a matter of only a few hundred dollars for this farmer, Andrew P. Kehoe, the monster responsible for killing some twenty-seven people, mostly children."

I paused to see their awe-struck faces that were now wide awake after hiking with Sleepy.

"You might ask, 'Why haven't I heard of this until now?' as I asked myself a few years ago. About the same time as this disaster, the Missouri River was flooding out thousands of people, and Charles Lindbergh was making his solo flight across the Atlantic. Plus, that was over seventy years ago, long before the media coverage of today. The details were in this out-of-print book. But I want to talk about my story and how I came to terms with even writing about such a thing. First off, I was invited to Bath, Michigan, by a man who lived there all his life and had told me in a letter where I could get a copy of this book about the disaster. Rather than go into all the details now, I decided to write about the disaster by turning it into historical fiction based on a true crime. And I changed the location of the disaster to Missouri because there were still survivors of the disaster living in the Bath, Michigan, area. Another reason I decided to write about this true crime is because I had talked quite a bit with the disaster's most scarred survivor, who was just a boy in the school when all hell broke loose on this little town. This incredible man encouraged me to write about that terrible event that changed his life forever. And there were a hundred little incredible things that happened while I was researching this disaster. One thing I will say about that gloomy

January and February in Michigan: I know for certain that there was an evil presence near me the deeper I got into this story. But I also know that I had some kind of invisible protection that compelled me to keep going and finish this book—mostly because in my imagination I had figured out how the town could get some kind of payback from that cowardly bastard who tried to destroy their little town by murdering their children."

After about twenty minutes at the podium going over this amazing back story I'd created in my reality, I asked my captivated audience if they had any questions. Every question was about the crime, the details, the stuff you would get from any newspaper or internet blurb today. They were not at all interested in what I had done—all the work and research it took to come out with the book I had displayed at the table next to me. It just seemed like once these tight-ass library book-signing attendees heard all the gruesome details, they just got up and left without buying my book. I couldn't believe it! I had given an outstanding presentation, and I had zero sales to show for it. I can still see them, their fat asses walking away from me and my book, some patting their wallets and looking guilty about leaving without buying my book. As an experienced salesman, I knew these people better than they ever thought I could. They were "the withholders," my potential readers, the same Americans who wonder why their kids have to move away from their tight-ass towns in order to start new lives somewhere. Anywhere, except where they were raised.

It must have been a day or two later, after the anger and disgust faded from that negative book-signing, that I got the worst phone call of my life. A policeman called to tell me that my brother had committed suicide. I knew that Kehoe—the evil coward of Bath, Michigan—had gotten back at me for exposing him in *Missouri Madness*. The same evil that compelled that monster to

71

murder so many innocent people had struck again when it told my brother's sick mind to do such a thing to himself and my family.

After getting lost in Germany for a couple weeks and seeing more of the same insanity over there, I moved away from North Carolina and eventually sold every damn copy of *Missouri Madness* to public libraries all over the country. In that novel I wanted people to know that evil spirits can possess people, and that it's widespread in America and manifest in every degree of insanity. That's what that fictional story was illustrating. Our towns and cities are saturated with the weak minds of cowards who are perpetrating all kinds of evil against people every day of every year. We are all influenced by it and even contribute to it by withholding love from others and ourselves.

Yes, book signings are a negative for me. But suit yourself.

Me all alone at a book signing.

Handling Rejection

This might be the most important chapter in the entire book for indie writers. I believe "Handling Rejection" should be taught as vigorously as any subject from grade school all the way through high school. Why? Look around you. We're all rejecting each other by ignoring the fact that we don't see rejection as a problem. If you're going to market your own writing, you'd better equip yourself with some tools you'll need to handle the rejection you'll get every day for the rest of your indie writing career. Even if you don't finish writing your book, you'll still need to handle rejection.

First off, let me say I'm not schooled with any kind of professional degree whatsoever. To me, that's a good thing in a system catering to a society that doesn't support art—unless it's a new concept for a beer commercial or graphic design for some pizza delivery box. If I sound jaded and cynical, it's because I am. I have been handling rejection since long before I published my first novel and sold ten thousand copies door to door. Rejection still bothers me today, but not on a personal level that causes me to doubt my work or diminishes my motivation. I get bothered by rejection when I don't sell many books in a day or if I'm getting skunked over a two- three- or even five-hour calling period. It's always important to me to get that first sale of the day under my belt to break the ice. Getting skunked sucks.

Rarely do I get skunked these days because my calls are a nice mix of cold-calls to libraries that don't shelve my books and calls to loyal repeat customers. With the economy down in the last decade, it sometimes has been tough to get more than three sales in a day. Even though I average five sales a day or one sale per hour, that's still a pretty slow per-hour selling rate when I think of what I used to do. When the economy was stronger, I was selling librarians an order for my books about every ten minutes. I was writing up six orders an hour versus the one sale per hour I average in today's economy. Man, that's a big difference! Occasionally I have days when sales are still that good, but those days are the exception rather than the rule in today's market. But believe me: When sales are going that well, selling time on the phone flies by. That's the time when the only thing that fatigues is my writing hand—from filling out so many invoices.

Fatigue will be an issue whenever you have long periods of zero sales. This is a good place to mention again that "good leads are glad you called." What I mean by that is: Once you have your perfect phone script down, all you have to do is keep accurate notes—particularly the librarian's first name and the response you get. Then keep dialing and listening for that one librarian who seems to be so easy to sell to. Believe me when I say there are librarians who will buy your book if you keep looking for them. It won't take you long to experience that if you don't give up.

While you're going through rejection you must take frequent breaks. Take a quick walk, do a few exercises, check the mail, play music you like; just do something to clear your head. Like a professional fighter you must rest between rounds before you get back out there to take your pounding from rejection. This is a good place to mention that you must have a telephone headset or earpiece so you can have your hands free; holding a phone to your ear is enervating after an hour or two. You should also be prepared to work on the phone from different places and bodily positions. For instance, I like to call prospects from my list while standing in front of a big window with a nice view that allows me to stretch my eyes and focus on other things besides small numbers on a page. I'll also walk around my apartment once I'm into a conversation about my books with a prospective librarian. Or I might lie on my back on my couch or my bed in order to elevate my legs on a cushion or a wall. If you like to work sitting down at a desk, make sure you have a solid-backed chair for support.

I save my back for writing, because that's when I sit down. I don't want to write after sitting all day and my back is killing me. If you do like to sit when you're on the phone, get up and move around often; otherwise you'll have a sore back and won't enjoy your work nearly as much. I have always gone to public places to write my first draft of a book. Writing in the morning when I'm fresh and later in the day after selling works best for me. That way I give myself two chances to move my story along. I know that if I take conscious care of my body while selling, I'll maintain my energy to write when I'm done selling for the day.

Getting in some exercise after calling, like a good long walk, always helps me shake off the rejection that always accumulates in my body. Since I'm sixty years old now, a short power nap helps me to recover and forget all the calls that ended in rejection. Maintaining a positive outlook and proactively caring for your body are the most powerful weapons for fighting the battle of rejection.

The reality of America in 2013 is that by far the number-one reason why you'll get rejected is "the lack of money." There is nothing you can do about the lack of money. The best approach you can take is to find out if and when the librarian or director wants you to call back and when she believes the money situation might be better. Make a note of it to call her back at that particular time. Some librarians I have been calling back as often as every six months and still getting the "no money" response. Unfortunately, libraries aren't funded during tough economic times like they are when the economy is good. To further complicate matters, when underfunded libraries finally get some money for books, they spend that money fast. Spurts of money dry up fast in libraries because they've been underfunded for so long and have a wish list of books—mostly bestsellers—that their patrons are requesting.

Librarians hate saying "no" because they love buying books for their patrons. So when they tell me they can't buy even one of my titles because of the lack of money, they feel as bad about the missed opportunity as the rejection does to me. Many times they feel even worse, because nobody really enjoys rejecting indie writers. Rejection hurts both ways.

I was going to have a chapter titled "Liars and Buyers," but that's too cynical—even for an indie writer like me. And yet it's true. There will be so many high school librarians who are so busy, they will pretend to write down your web page and tell you they will contact you if interested. There is an easy way to root out the buyers from the liars: Just ask them point blank, either before or after you give them your web page, "Can I call you back soon to see if you're interested in my book?" If the answer is yes, find out when you can call the librarian back. It's a good lead. If she says "No, I'll contact you later if I'm interested," you may as well mark that library as a "No" because 99 out of 99 will never contact you. But at least the next time you call, you'll have the librarian's name and know that you left your web page.

If I still have inventory left of the same book or if I have published a new book (or even both), I'll call that same school library the next school year and hope there's a new librarian who's doing the buying. Many times I have called back and sold my books to a new librarian who really was glad I called. Sometimes even the same librarian who had to turn me down earlier will buy my book after a second contact. More often, though, I prefer it when a new person is doing the buying because my chances are much improved. In defense of librarians who reject you, usually it is genuinely because of lack of money.

It will take about twenty days of calling (or about a month) to reach the point where rejection doesn't bother you and sales are good enough to reassure you that you're on the right track. So after a month of consistent calling, you will be a successful writer, having placed your books on the shelves of libraries where they could be circulating long after you are but a memory. So make your writing count by continuing to put it out there. With consistent daily reading, writing, and marketing of your work Monday through Friday, at least four to five hours a day, you will become a "real" writer with new readers every day of the year reading your book all over the country.

As a general rule, it doesn't pay to call public libraries on the weekend, unless it's a really small library and that's the only time to reach the librarian who buys the books. Most librarians, library directors, and acquisition personnel don't work on weekends. If they do (as is the case with some smaller libraries), they're usually pretty busy and for the most part don't like talking to authors about their books. After you have been calling for some time, you will find that you have accumulated several little libraries where the buyer is in on Saturdays. It may be best to devote one Saturday to calling all of those libraries while taking another day off during the week. I have come to learn that it is important to have two days off, away from the phone, so you can come back fresh Monday morning. Even shortening your hours or taking Friday off is a good idea if you can afford it. Friday will be your slowest sales day of the work week.

Another fun but sometimes discouraging part of marketing your own book is having readers contact you at your email address. Mine is always printed on or near the last page of the book. The positive feedback will motivate you for several days and will put a spring in your step that only edification from your readers can give you. But then there's the other side. Teachers, librarians, English majors, Amazon book reviewers (hacks), and avid readers will at one time or another criticize your writing to the point that it might put a damper on marketing your book—but only for a day or two. Much of the criticism of your writing will be fair; and if taken with a positive attitude, it will compel you to improve your work and you'll see the results with your next book.

One memorable and funny example of a shocking negative response from a young reader came to me on my voicemail sometime in 2001. (This incident taught me to *never* put my phone number or physical mailing address on my books. I only use a post office box and email address.) I had been selling my novel *Autumn Letters* to high schools in the Bronx—one of the toughest school districts in the country—so I knew right away where this kid was from when I listened to my voice mail. This kid was ranting on and on about what a terrible writer I was, using expletives, wrath and enmity the likes of which I'd never experienced before or since from one of my readers. But then I realized how I really reached that kid with my writing, for better or for worse, to a degree that had moved and motivated him to call me and give me such a tongue-lashing. For me, I easily turned that negative experience into a positive one just because I was by then inured to handling rejection.

So you indie writers out there who are still reading this book: Keep reading, writing, and be willing to take the negative stuff and turn it into a positive when marketing your writing to the world—one library at a time.

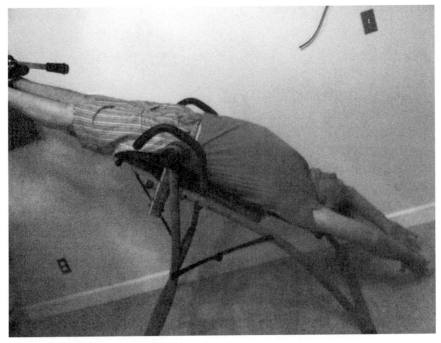

Me on my trusty Teeter!

Your Covers

The front and back covers are the most important marketing aspects of your book and deserve the most attention. Since you're not anybody's favorite writer yet (except maybe your mother's), an indie writer must have a striking cover to get the reader's attention. I found this out the hard way when my librarians told me my early titles were not being checked out of their libraries because they believed my covers were not getting much attention from their patrons.

Unfortunately, they were right; yet I still had thousands of books to sell on my shoestring budget. It was a substantially higher price to add two colors to my covers, so I opted to go with a simpler, one-color cover. Yes, it was the same "lack of money" that kept me in the lower circulating ranks of indie writers peddling their book.

Looking back with the advantage of knowledge that comes with experience and maturity, I have to admit there was a part of me that didn't want the attention a great cover would get when I knew that my editing and writing capabilities were subpar. In other words, I didn't want a great cover to bring more criticism from more readers.

My girlfriend made an interesting point regarding covers: "Books are looked at like people are looked at; we judge them by their cover."

Sadly, it's true. We don't pick up books by indie writers and look them over until we've judged the cover, much like we do with people. We judge them by what we see on the outside and then decide whether we want to look further.

A potential reader will judge your book by its cover. Ask any librarian and she will tell you it's true. Now I spend much more time thinking about my covers. Luckily I have an artist named Tony Conrad in Sioux Falls, South Dakota, who gives me a fair price for great covers. And he's fast. It seems that the best artists and professionals in any field are quick about getting their work done. So find someone in your area who is known to be a good artist capable of designing the look for your covers that you want. Usually printers who can put a book together know of local artists you can contact. Personally, I know you can save money by having your own artist who can provide your cover art to your printer.

Also, you will need a UPC-13 ISBN barcode printed on the lower right corner of your back cover so that library staff and most retailers can scan your title into their system. I use a company called Symbology. There's a modest charge for the barcode numbers and film that they will ship directly to your printer to put on your new title.

There's another barcode used by large retailers like Barnes and Noble or Borders that they require for their scanning, and they want that barcode placed on the inside front cover. I don't want to place my titles in these bigger bookstores because they want my books on consignment, and they want me to pay the shipping to get them there. Then every three months they will send me my percentage for each book they sell. Personally, I don't want anything to do with tracking my sales and having my inventory tied up by some giant corporation. That's a good way to go broke and not a practical, proactive way to market your book.

Ultimately, it's up to you. Your barcode company will help you and let you know what you should have for barcoding when you let them know who you want to sell your books to.

Again, people really do judge a book by its cover; so make your covers as striking, appealing and attractive as possible. Look at other book covers and ask your friends and even random potential readers for their feedback when you have the artwork ready for your covers.

You can see some of my more recent front covers. The back cover is not as visually important as the front cover, yet I believe that the text on the back cover will make a big difference whether a reader checks out or buys your book. Since you're an indie writer, reviews won't matter much to open-minded readers who are willing to give an indie writer a read. Readers want to know what the story is about. The cover and your text on the back cover should convey the genre or type of story you've written. Put time into your book cover's text, and keep making your covers as compelling as possible.

My first cover of Ledges (yes it was this blurry) Ledges now.

Which one do you think looks better?

Calling Canada

In two important ways, calling libraries in Canada is a welcomed oasis for me. It increases my prospects by ten percent, and the librarians seem to be less rushed and have more patience and time to talk when I call. Canadian public libraries are listed in the second book of the two-volume *American Library Directory*. They are alphabetized by provinces with the same time zones as in the United States. I suggest you call all the provinces except Quebec, since libraries there are more inclined to buy French titles.

The cell phone companies I have dealt with don't have unlimited calling plans that include Canada. It's too expensive per minute and stressful unless you have an unlimited calling plan with your cable company like I've always had with my home phone service. I would only use my cell phone for calling if my service provider would let me call Canada without a per-minute charge, which is not an option for me at this time. Every day throughout the year I like to mix it up and make some calls from my RV or from a coffeehouse where I write, but I always have to call Canada from my home.

There are a few negatives to calling Canada. The postage by United States Postal Service to Canada is much higher, depending on the weight of your book. I average about $2.00 to $3.00 in the U.S. by media mail, but it jumps considerably whenever I ship my books to Canada. It's more of a hassle postage-wise whenever I ship three or four books at a time to a Canadian library. The postage is around $12.00 compared to the $3.00- to $4.00-range in the U.S. It's a good idea to go to your post office and find out your shipping costs to Canada before you start selling to our neighbors up north.

Another negative is you must fill out a USPS Customs Declaration form with every order you ship to Canada. It is easy, however, once you are used to filling out this form. And the time a postal clerk takes to fill out all the required information requires patience.

Still another negative is that Canadian libraries like to pay me in Canadian funds. They don't want the hassle of getting a U.S. money order. That's why I always mark "CA $" on my invoice and highlight it, since I've told the librarian in my sales pitch that my book is priced in Canadian dollars to make it easier for her to pay me.

Keep in mind that you will need to price your book a few dollars more to cover the higher postage and the lower exchange rate. For example, a $20.00 "CA $" might be $19.20 when the exchange rate is converted at your bank. Also, my bank charges me $1.50 to convert my Canadian checks to U.S. dollars. I suggest you price your book $4.00 to $5.00 higher to cover postage, the exchange rate, and any bank charges.

These are all fixed expenses you have to consider in order to accurately price your book when calling Canadian libraries. Overall, I have found these extra charges to be worth the trouble in order to get my books placed in Canadian libraries when libraries in the U.S. are so tight for money. Libraries in Canada are just as strapped for funds as U.S. libraries, yet it's a bit easier to call libraries up north because they don't get called as much by authors. New territory should be a nice respite for you and should help you move your inventory.

Another note about Canadian public libraries: Many are closed on Mondays, but not all of them.

I've never bought a list of Canadian high schools to market my books. It's been easier to do things the hard way when my cost per book goes up in Canada. While prospecting Canadian libraries, I have been able to get the names and phone numbers of high schools near that particular public library from their local directory. It wasn't much of a hassle since librarians in the U.S. and Canada are incredibly accommodating about looking up phone numbers fast—if they're not too busy when you call. Labor-intensive calling like that is behind me now, and so are the lessons learned. My best advice to you is to buy a list of schools in the U.S. and Canada.

For some reason I have noticed that Canadian high schools have more mature readers than U.S. high schools. Personally, I believe Canada is a more open-minded society because they have ten percent of our population. More people equals more problems.

If you decide to call libraries to the north, you will find that Canadians love Americans and will buy your book just as easily as U.S. libraries. Canadian librarians are well aware of your increased expenses, so don't be shy about marking up your book as mentioned previously. Canadians love American writers too.

Little Things Matter

Like all small businesses, indie writers have to keep track of expenses related to writing and publishing their books. Here is a list of most of the expenses that have to be tracked for your tax forms:

- Editing services
- Printing costs
- Freight (if any)
- Artwork for covers
- Copies
- Postage
- Shipping bags
- Invoices
- Rubber stamps for invoices and bags (such as your return address or "media mail")
- Gas
- Meals
- Lodging (such as for book signings)
- Expenses related to travel when researching and selling your book on the road
- Phone (if you sell your books via telemarketing)
- Copyrights
- Storage for books
- Rent for office space or home office deduction (see tax forms)

I'm no tax expert, but I do know what I can and cannot write off as expenses related to my writing. I'm not about to list every little expense you might incur related to your writing, but pay attention to your expenses. Save your receipts and consult your accountant or the IRS tax guides for the expenses you are allowed to claim.

Many libraries, both public and school, will request a W-9 form from you for their records. They want your tax identification number or social security number. Some will request this and send you a copy of a W-9 form to fill out and return to them before they pay you for your book. Keep copies on hand of W-9 forms because just when you think they've sent you a check, you open the envelope and there's a W-9 form instead. These forms can be accessed and downloaded from the IRS website, www.irs.gov. It's an easy federal form to fill out, so get it back in the mail in order to get paid. Since I have moved often in my writing career to research my books, many of my librarians who know me will send a check with a new W-9. I really appreciate that.

Vendor forms are short forms a school district or public library wants filled out so that you are a registered vendor doing business with their city, county, or state entity. I find that previous incompetence, corruption, collusion and mismanaged funds are the reasons for most vendor forms. They are trying to keep their money straight so that crooks are not getting paid for services. Just fill out the form and know that it's part of doing business with government entities.

There's no getting around purchase orders when you sell your books to libraries, especially public schools. Purchase orders are used by librarians who have to requisition and fill out a form to get money to buy books. These days it seems that somebody has to approve spending money for anything. A poor economy hurts libraries more than it should. (Easy for me to say when I rely on libraries to buy my books.)

There's an easy way to ship my books—if the librarian is willing—before the purchase order is requisitioned, and that is to send them with an open or undated invoice. Of course, the librarian usually knows me or at least knows that funds for buying books will be available soon, or else she wouldn't let me send my books that way. She just fills in the date after she has received my books and when she has her purchase order in the works. That way my invoice date doesn't predate her purchase order requisition date. And since libraries are tax exempt, you don't have to charge sales tax on your invoice.

As much as possible, I try to use the poor economy to my advantage since at this time I'm in the throes of selling my three new titles. (See my web page www.michaelfrederick82.com.) During this slow period, I'm selling my last two titles remaining in my inventory to libraries interested in door prize giveaways for upcoming events. I'm marketing them two of each for $8.00 a copy or four books for $32.00. Of course I sign them, and it really helps move my remaining inventory. Many of the libraries don't want to give away books, though, because they usually give out prizes that were donated to them.

While in the throes of pre-selling my new titles, I have to keep moving inventory to libraries that don't have my last two titles. I offer them my last two books at $16.00 each and donate a matching set, so again it's a $32.00 invoice. That way the free books can be given away as door prizes, and I have a good shot at selling the librarian my new books closer to my publishing date October 1st.

Since I'm an unknown indie writer out of the conventional publishing loop and without a distributor, I must be aggressive on the phone and press until I find a librarian willing to get my books now. Luckily, I seem to always find them. And so will you after a little experience and coaching from me, if needed. I know that if you're like me, you'll try this on your own to see how you do. Just know that I'm an email away from helping you. And I realize that very few of you will even attempt this arduous way of putting your work out there.

Regarding accounts payable: If you haven't been paid after the thirty-day period as noted on your invoice, I would call the librarian who ordered your book. She will usually be the best resource for looking into the late invoice you sent her.
Often enough they will lose your invoice, and you can email the librarian a copy of it. It is always frustrating to call a librarian or accounts payable person in a school to see if my invoice is "in the works to be paid." This collecting is part of any business and is necessary in about five percent of your sales. Also, it's possible that the post office didn't even get your books there, and that's the reason they're losing more customers every year.

The real problem regarding a late invoice is, as previously stated, the lack of money. Board meetings can fall on a date when you have to wait for about two months before getting paid. That's part of the reality of doing business with public libraries. Most librarians are good about getting your invoice paid on time. As with everything in life, it's that one percent that keeps anything from being perfect and where patience is needed.

Proofing or reading your manuscript before it's published is worth mentioning here. Words get repeated and dozens of errors show up even after your editor has proofed it. Read your final draft that's been proofed by your editor and you'll be amazed at the errors you both missed. Once you sign off on the publisher's proof, any mistakes you have missed will be out there on library shelves for many years. And trust me, your readers will let you know about them. I have had letters and emails where readers have pointed out typos and other mistakes, and that was it. Nothing else. Editors are good, but they miss things. And it isn't your printer's job to edit your book. It's a good idea to have a friend read your final proof. You'll be amazed at the mistakes a fresh pair of eyes will find.

As you can see on the back cover of this book, I put the vinyl lettering "Don't Read My Books" with my website address on the back of my RV. At first I had "Read My Books" with the website, thinking and hoping I would get sales from thousands of miles I'd travel on my book-selling summer runs in the Midwest that would last four to five days. Wrong! At the very least it angered other travelers because "Read My Books" was like an order from some pest who was going fifty-five miles an hour and hindering their progress. I can't say it even sold one book for me.

I really put the signage to a test when my girlfriend and I went on an extended book-selling tour from Omaha to Phoenix, then further west to San Diego and all the way up the California coast into Oregon and back to Omaha. At eight miles per gallon, it was an expensive trip while we enjoyed the incredible scenery far removed from Nebraska. On this long trip I sold books here and there to retailers I called before we left Omaha. When you drive an RV, you eventually end up with traffic backed up behind you in construction zones or in areas of high elevation where passing is prohibited. I could just sense that my signage and command to "Read My Books" and web address was resented by angry drivers in a hurry, and I seemed to be cramming my books down their throats. After such a long trip with literally thousands of passing vehicles, I was disappointed when I only got one response from a driver in Ventura, California. And he didn't even buy one book.

So then I had an idea: Instead of removing the signage, I added "Don't" to the front of my command, cynically using reverse psychology with the new command "Don't Read My Books." I figured if nothing else, that would at least be a different approach. Believe me, it works. There are a thousand little things I do without realizing I do them, just because I'm an American writer who knows that "writing" is ninety percent marketing.

Your Second Book

Even while I was waiting for my first novel to be printed, I was writing my second novel. This is an anxious period because you won't know for sure if you can consistently sell your first book until you're doing it. And once you do start moving your inventory, it won't take you long to figure out when you'll be sold out of your first book. My point is: Don't wait until your first book is completely sold out before you publish your second book.

I didn't see my economic security until I started selling two books together. Now I can take two years to write two new titles, no matter what my inventory level is. Many times I have found myself selling three, four or even five books at a time until my inventory was reduced to selling only my last two titles. One book, or a twenty-dollar invoice, just doesn't add up unless you're consistently selling fifteen to twenty orders a day. Selling days like that are down the road and out of sight in this economy for a new writer who doesn't have a bunch of loyal readers in libraries yet. It takes time to get loyal readers.

After a year of selling my new books, I start calling my oldest and best public libraries in December or the second day of the new year, selling my two new titles that will be shipped October 1st—some nine to ten months away. I do this every two years. The first year I concentrate on writing the first book while still selling my inventory. The second year I work on writing my second new title. I try to have them finished in plenty of time for my editor while selling my inventory down as low as possible so I'm not selling four or five books at a time for long. That's why I reduce the prices of my inventory to move them along.

During this preselling calling period for my new titles, I am also making calls here and there selling new libraries my reduced inventory. These are libraries that have never carried my titles or libraries that bought earlier books that they weeded out because their patrons just didn't read them. These inventory sales are important because they pay the monthly bills.

For you writers who have another job to pay the bills and don't like my aggressive marketing approach, you can take your time and call high school librarians and let them know you are interested in author chats via webcam. Schools don't have much of a budget for this; however, students have spending money and you can sell your books to them this way to move your inventory. Of course, your book has to be geared for them; it's just too soft of an approach for me with a high probability of no sales for long periods of time. Your schedule has to be incredibly flexible to do these author chats. They are certainly not for me.

I'll back up and emphasize this: You'll find it easier to sustain a living if you sell two books at a time versus one. This is another reason you'll most likely need some consulting along the way. I can help you make (or help save you) thousands of dollars whether you self-publish your book or not. I'm sure many of you started reading this and decided it was too much work. Well, you're welcome. Down the road you'll see that I saved you a bunch of time and money by telling you these things about self-publishing. Today, writing is ninety percent marketing and ten percent writing for those of you who want to stay clear of conventional publishing. This may seem like a much more difficult way to put your work out there, but it's not. Waiting to be validated by a bunch of lawyers and agents who only want a piece of your work is actually much harder.

Now that you've finished writing your second book, you're ready to have your editor and printer correct all the mistakes you made with your first book. Maybe the font size was too small on your first title or the chapter titles weren't positioned where you now know you'd like them to be, or now you're anxious to have your margins moved a bit. Unlike me, my books get better looking with time. And now I'm certain that I have to make my words on my first page of my second book as enticing as I can. Maybe on your second book you'll want your artist to put drawings on your chapter title pages.

If you have inventory left, you will now be able to make a better living for yourself by selling two titles to libraries. Again, I would stay away from the bigger libraries and their red tape. Librarians like to look at your books on your web page, so now you'll have two titles to show them. Right away on the phone ask the busy librarian if she can take a quick look at your web page NOW. This way you can sell your books now—not later. Trust me: they won't buy your books later.

When you call, if the librarian is not by a computer or is too busy at that moment to look at your web page, ask the librarian when you can call back to see if she'll buy your books (or your new title if she has your first book). It's not a good idea to leave it up to the librarian to call you back or contact you on your web page. Ninety-nine times out of a hundred she won't. She's too busy. Unless she has patrons requesting your second title, you'd better plan to call her back.

Here's something I didn't do on my second book that you should do when you're calling back your libraries that have your first title. First off, the librarian will look right away at your circulation figures in her system. This is the anxious time to cross your fingers and hope that your first book had more than a few readers since your book has been shelved at that library. If your book only had one or two or even zero check-outs, it doesn't bode well for you as she will be less likely to buy your second title. But be ready. She may ask you about your second book or decide to look at your second book on your web site now. If the librarian doesn't buy your second book, then let her know you'll call her back in six months to see if your circulation has improved. If she has seen some check-outs, she may give your second book a chance. I'm getting pretty good at picking up quick, just by a librarian's tone of voice, whether or not my books have circulated as soon as she knows who I am.

Either way, here's what you have to be ready for: Positive comments the librarian may say because she read your book and really enjoyed it, or a patron or two who may have made positive comments about your book. This is the time to sell your second book to her after telling her about it. It is also the perfect time to ask the librarian or director if you can quote her on your website. For example: "My patrons are enjoying Michael's first novel *Ledges*—Mary Jones, Librarian at Hayes Public Library in Hayes, Kansas." Don't ask Mary to send you an email of her quote to put on your website. Mary's too busy for that. Take over and ask her NOW if you can put her positive quote on your website. Since chances are you won't get professional reviews from source books, these positive quotes you get from your librarians can mean the difference between selling a book or two and not. So, once again, if you're fortunate enough to hear from a librarian that your first book has been circulating well in her library, ask her right then if you can use her name and quote on your website.

The same is true for your readers who send you positive feedback. Email or ask your reader on the phone if you can put her positive feedback about your book on your website. It's best to use first names only. These positive quotes will help you with your sales, and they are even better if they are from a librarian or teacher.

You have to really listen for these positive words or even a receptive voice of a librarian, because she could be telling you that "your books are really being enjoyed by our patrons." So ask how your books are doing and be ready to ask for a little help with your self-promoting. I think most of us have trouble asking for help when it comes to putting our work out there.

EBooks may seem like the easier way to go, since you can download your book on Amazon with their step-by-step process. Doing so will make you think that now the world is going to come after your writing. Yeah, right. That's the lazy way that won't move your inventory.

You'll see that your first book has taught you more things about writing and marketing your second book. I know that your second book will prove to you that you are an indie writer who is now making a good living doing what you love—and getting better all the time. By now you're more comfortable writing every day; and as an indie writer marketing two books to libraries, you feel that the stress from lack of money has diminished considerably. Yes, I know what you're thinking now:
What about other markets, where readers could see my books in stores and buy them?

Retail

At this point it's not for me. I've tried it. Several times. I've sold my books to chain and indie bookstores, gift shops, grocery stores and drugstores, truck stops and convenience stores, florist and beauty shops, coffeehouses, etc. Of course, I had to sell them for less money because they would buy multiple copies—up to two dozen at a time. I did this to move my inventory and to see if the retail market would buy my signed book when they saw it in a store. I needed to see if I was missing out on the "buying" public.

Now I know I was one of those items in a store that didn't move fast enough for my retailers. Much later, when I would call my retail outlets, most of the time I would hear that my books just weren't selling fast enough in order to get repeat orders. I was counting on my budget-conscious library readers to either buy my signed books, or that I could at least get some word-of-mouth sales from my loyal readers in libraries. It didn't happen. Yet that doesn't mean I haven't had some retailers here and there sell my books pretty fast and order my new titles when I'd call them several months later, or in some cases over a year later. Except for allowing me to move some inventory, retail was and is a big disappointment for me.

Additionally, even though my books always have my contact information on the back page, I can't recall many retailers contacting me about reordering my books for their customers.

I have heard time and again from retailers that my books don't sell, and they don't want to buy any to replace what have been sold. That first sale to the retailer was the easiest because I signed one of the personalized copies to the buyer or to someone else the buyer wanted to give a copy to. This was a good way to get things started, and yet sales were never good enough to get easy reorders. I'd get employees here and there that read and enjoyed my books, but still not enough to spark other sales from the public.

What I interpreted from these poor sales in retail outlets over and over again was that my books aren't good enough. I knew to a certain extent that was true, yet I had to keep writing and selling my inventory.

Preselling my new titles every two years to my loyal libraries reenergizes me to no end because I keep hearing positive feedback from animated, friendly people who buy my new books without much concern for what they are about or how much they cost. I love that.

The best example of how I put my heart into retail early was in the first part of this century when I got a phone list of all the Hy-Vee stores in the Midwest. Hy-Vee is the country's largest independently owned grocery store. Over two hundred stores bought my second printing of *Ledges*. Still, the public was not buying my book at a good enough clip to get repeat orders. Most of the stores would eventually sell them all. Some stores had to "clearance price" them to get rid of them, and some of the stores wanted a refund since I "guaranteed" my books (as long as the books were in good condition and I could resell them). This was always a point of contention from my point of view since I had to resell them. I still shop at Hy-Vee every week, and I don't bring back goods I haven't used and ask for a refund six months later.

In 2012 I was still selling my new titles to Hy-Vee stores, yet not to nearly as many stores since a good percentage of them have given up on my books as a product that will move for them. I can't blame them. At least they gave my books a chance, and that's why I'm still a loyal customer of theirs today.

All this unpredictability from the buying public is why I'm not placing my new titles in any retail outlets. Not only would it be tough selling finding stores here and there that would buy my books, but it's just too much of a hassle and a downer to see my books collecting dust in these stores. This way, at least I can tell librarians (if they ask) that my books are sold exclusively to libraries.

As recently as the summer of 2012, I'd be out on the road selling my books direct after pre-calling prospects, as well as stopping in to pitch "cold" prospects. That's when I'd find that some of my books sold five to ten years back were still there unsold, and I'd end up replacing them with newer titles just to get new books out there. That's embarrassing. And unprofitable.

Of course, these experiences I have had are relative to my writing ability. Your writing may be far superior to mine, so you have to take that into consideration when reading about my experiences selling my work. Look at it as a warning of what you may face. But then realize that when one book fails to sell or circulate well, we always get a new chance with a new book. That's part of the trap that made me try again at retail: "Maybe they'll like this one."

There are two more reasons grocery stores and drugstores are not a good outlet for books for indie writers. First, space is at a premium. Secondly, many stores have an outside distributor who handles their books and magazines, making it difficult to place your indie title in their racks that the distributor wants filled with their merchandise.

If you really want to test the retail market, do it in your immediate area and see how your book sells. Again, if you're like me and the retail buying public in your area doesn't support you, you may want to move. Far away.

In closing this chapter, I want to say that there is more positive than negative in most things related to indie publishing and marketing, except for the retail aspect. It takes patience and money to play the withholding game that retail demands of indie writers. I understand why. It's because there's more and more crap written by indie writers. Anyone can publish a book these days, and it won't necessarily be anything worth reading. Just beware of retail.

Hit the Road

When you're getting bored and tired of calling prospects when marketing your book—and you will—plan a road trip. Go somewhere new. It doesn't have to be far away. Now and then I like to get away in my RV during the week and do my calling from new restaurants and coffeehouses along the way. Soon you'll discover that your sales haven't dropped off, and you're putting new life into your marketing and your writing. All of this is good because you've managed to change your environment without hurting your income.

There's nothing quite like a good road trip to clear out the cobwebs for a writer. You'll see your characters in a new light that brings about new obstacles and resolutions, breathing new energy into your book. Of course the energy has to come from you, the writer.

On your road trip, if you're outgoing you could sell your book along the way to waitresses and motel clerks or anyone you happen to meet along your trip. Last summer I mapped out a scenic route in my atlas. I researched the phone numbers of retailers along the way and called them, letting the buyers know I was coming to their town and wanted to stop by to show them my novels. I sold enough books here and there to help offset expenses, and I was able to write the whole trip off as a bookselling tour. I have learned from experience that sometimes my prospects are not at the store when I happen to hit their town, so I would usually give a quick call when I knew I could stop to show my books. I have found that many buyers are willing to try a half-dozen copies of my books. Of course, you'll want to make a few bucks a copy and yet price your book low enough that your prospective retailer can make a few bucks, too. Keep in mind that consumers won't pay more for your paperback book than they would for the mainstream bestsellers.

When you do sell your book to retailers or readers on the road, ask them for feedback. Ask them to contact you via your email address located at the back of your book. This is a good way to get a real feel for your writing. If a reader really likes your book, you may hear something. Chances are if your reader didn't like your book and/or might have particular criticisms, you won't hear from that reader. This is the real world of an indie writer: usually hearing nothing from your readers in a world too busy to respond. Being ignored is something indie writers have to get used to, even though it's just the opposite of why we risk ourselves by putting our writing out into the world. It can be scary.

Hitting the road and pitching your books to strangers is easier than selling your book in familiar territory. Trust me. After marketing a book or two for some time, you'll realize that it's just plain good for your spirit to get away for a few days. And if during this getaway you don't even sell one book, at least spend more time writing your next book. Believe it or not, writing more pages of your next book is money down the road and often worth much more than the paltry sales you managed that drained your writing energy that day.

Like every small business venture, it doesn't take a mental giant to figure out how much money you make per page after a sustained period of selling your book or books. That's why I'm always torn between publishing more books every two years or focusing on just one good one. Nevertheless, hitting the road and writing in a new environment is the best thing you can do for your writing.

On the road when I was younger, selling was always my priority and writing was secondary. Today that is reversed because now I know that more money comes in with more pages. I used to exhaust myself selling like some crazed lunatic all day long to anyone in my path. Then I'd be bothered all night that I didn't have any energy to write. Now I balance it out. Make time to write. Both sales and new pages will come if you're consistent.

Picking up Traveller and getting ready to hit the road!

Training for SLUGS

Somebody Living Under Great Stress. That's what the acronym SLUGS stands for. I respectfully began calling telemarketers "slugs" years ago, but now I know it can also refer to anyone working and/or living in America.

As in my fifteenth title and fourteenth novel *King of Slugs,* working people today are slugs. If you decide to be an indie writer and market your book, sales and marketing will take up ninety percent of your time. And if you decide to use the telephone, like a million other slugs you will be traveling at the speed of sound. You will be making your living in a way that's on the same short list as other such despised professions: car salesmen, lawyers, doctors and bankers. Of these professions, the phone slugs or telemarketers are by far the least paid and the least appreciated, even though they outnumber all the other despised professionals by a thousand to one. I have often wondered why that is since I know phone slugs move more products and services than any other profession on the planet. I include in this number the growing contingent of slugs who sell and market products and services using the internet.

Slugs get very little positive attention anywhere, despite being an incredibly important part of our workforce and economy. I'm not talking about those unprofessional slugs who use the phone for deleterious scams and have Spam for brains. Those idiots are just criminals who use the phone. Those kinds of rats hide behind the phone and give the rest of us slugs a bad rap.

Every day I set a goal to have not one single librarian or director upset with my call and approach. Most days I can; some days I can't. There are times when I call a librarian who has a policy never to buy anything on the phone. Ever! And she won't. So I can only tell her, "I appreciate checking with you," and mark that library in the directory "NO PH." My only chance to sell that particular library is if a new librarian will be there when I call back in a couple years. Usually the same librarian is there for eternity. Yet several times I have sold that same library later because there's a new agent who buys, and she buys three or four of my books. My point is: Don't give up on libraries where a certain librarian doesn't like or appreciate phone sales made by an indie writer. Good things will happen if you stay positive and keep calling.

This book has been a training manual for slugs—one indie writer's attempt to instill in newbie indies the reality today that writing is ninety percent marketing. Since I want to (and must) work, there is no better work than spending my time putting my writing out there. I have a voice and a desire to tell a story and find my readers one at a time.

My goal writing this book has been to save you time and money. There will be some of you who will market your book your way after reading this. There is nobody to compete with; just you and your persistent passion to be a published indie writer—even if that means you sell every book you print at swap meets. Most of you will not want to publish "the hard way" as I have. Either way, I have saved you a bunch of time and money. You're welcome.